Janis Balodis trained at Town [illegible] majoring in drama, and worl[illegible] teacher until 1972. He then [illegible] directing career based in [illegible] London. He was Director and [illegible] at the E15 acting school.

His first play, *Backyard* was workshopped at the 1980 Australian National Playwrights Conference and produced at the Nimrod Theatre. In 1982 he was commissioned to write a play based on Northern Territory history for the Darwin Theatre Group, this resulted in *Beginning of the End* which toured successfully. *Too Young for Ghosts* was commissioned by the Sydney Theatre Company; productions opened at the Melbourne Theatre Company, the Stage Company Adelaide and the Drama Theatre, Sydney in 1985. *Wet and Dry* was completed for the Darwin Theatre Group in the same year. He was commissioned by the State Theatre Company of South Australia to write a play for the 1988 Bicentennial - *Heart for the Future* which premiered with the Melbourne Theatre Company as its 500th production at the Playhouse. He has also written plays for television and has developed the screenplay of *Backyard*

Janis Balodis has been Associate Director of the Melbourne Theatre Company since 1988.

Too Young For GHOSTS

JANIS BALODIS

CURRENCY PRESS • SYDNEY

CURRENCY PLAYS
General Editor: Katharine Brisbane

First published in 1991
by Currency Press Pty Ltd
P.O. Box 452, Paddington NSW 2021
Australia.

National Library of Australia
Cataloguing-in-Publication data
Balodis, Janis.
Too young for ghosts
ISBN 0 86819 281 3
I. Title.
A822.3

Typeset by Allette Systems Pty Ltd, Sydney
Printed by Australian Print Group, Maryborough, Vic

Cover photo shows Carlton Lamb as Leichhardt and Neil Modra as Gilberts in the NIDA final year student production directed by Terence Clarke at the Parade Theatre, June 1989. Photographer: Marco Bok.

Contents

Above: Denis Moore as Edvards, Mary Sitarenos as Ruth, Geoff Revell as Otto, Robynne Bourne as Lydia, Brandon Burke as Karl, Pamela Rabe as Ilse. Melbourne Theatre Company production 1985. Photo: David Parker. Below: Ailsa Piper as Ilsa and Craig Ashley as G.I.Joe. Sydney Theatre Company production 1985. Photo: Andrew Southam.

The Post-War Australian Immigrant Experience

What does a party of men led by Leichhardt exploring Northern Queensland in the late 1840's have in common with a group of Latvian immigrants coming to terms with life as casual workers in the same ancient land almost a century later? Most of us would say, nothing. But for Janis Balodis their comparative experiences provide an interesting backdrop to examine the complexities of the phenomenon of migration, and of the human spirit seeking to conquer hardship brought about by physical and social alienation.

In his play, *Too Young For Ghosts,* Janis Balodis explores a range of similarities between the attempts by Leichhardt and his party to come to terms with the mysteries of an ancient Aboriginal land little appreciated by the explorers interested only in fame and fortune, and the struggle of the Latvians to understand their new social environment which while providing them with many opportunities also diminishes their sense of pride and self-confidence.

The Latvians of whose story Balodis tells came to Australia as part of a migration program, the scope of which has few parallels. The origins of this program lay mostly in the political changes caused by the Second World War. For Australia, the war had led it to the realisation that its small population was vulnerable to external military aggression. The popular thinking of the time was encapsulated in the phrase, 'populate or perish'. And in order to 'populate', an extensive program of economic reconstruction and development was needed. And since an expanded labour force could not be achieved through natural growth, a more robust immigration program seemed like the only viable option.

For almost a century, immigration to Australia had been highly selective with most of the new settlers coming from the British Isles. But when this source could not provide sufficient numbers the country had to look elsewhere. One such source was to be found in the refugee camps of war-torn Europe. In those camps lived literally millions of displaced people, thrown out of their own native lands, desperate to make new lives. Most dreamt of eventually settling in the United States of America; but failing this, they readily accepted the prospect of emigrating to Australia. Their image of Australia was of a frontier land that provided many opportunities for those who were prepared to work hard. Australians, they had imagined, were a happy go lucky people - honest, open-minded and tolerant. But for most refugees in Australia the reality turned out to be very different. They found Australia to possess a culture of entrenched xenophobia. It is the manner in which a group of Latvian Displaced Persons coped with this culture that is the central theme of Balodis's play.

Between 1947 and 1953, 170 000 European refugees arrived in Australia. Of these, some 9 000 were Latvians, who, like all other Displaced Persons, had to complete a two year bond, working wherever the Australian government chose to send them. They were required to work long hours, often in conditions that few Australians would have tolerated. Those who objected were threatened with deportation by the authoritarian immigration officials, and the employers made little attempt to understand their traditions and personal histories.

The Displaced Persons, it must be remembered, had already experienced considerable hardship in the German refugee camps. But for many, things got worse in Australia; the camps at Wagga, Cowra, Bonegilla, Rushworth and the like provided an even more regimented and oppressive social environment. Not surprisingly, they readily accepted any job outside the camps they were offered, even when they knew little of where they were being sent. From Bonegilla, a large number of refugees were sent to the cane-cutting fields of Northern Queensland. Gangs were formed by nationality which included the Italians, the Spanish, the Lithuanians, and of course the Latvians.

The working conditions in the cane fields were harsh in the extreme, especially for these men who were brought up in the cold climate of Europe. The hot sun, the insects, the black soot of the burnt cane and the back-breaking work over as many as twelve hours a day, often resulted in infected blisters, sugar-cane fever and dysentry. The lack of medical care and primitive living conditions added to their woes. Home was a galvanised iron shed with little light or ventilation. Food was often supplied by the farmers, and was very basic. Sundays were the only day that provided some respite when there was at least an opportunity to cook their own food and relax by the beach or the river.

The problems that the Latvians confronted were compounded by the fact that most Australians were as ignorant about the refugees as the Latvians were about Australia before their arrival. Despite the reluctance of most Australians to take the kinds of jobs that the refugees accepted, there was considerable hostility about them 'taking our jobs'. Derogatory terms such as 'Reffos', 'Bloody Balts' and 'DPs' were frequently used to refer to all refugees. Many Latvians were moreover falsely accused of being fascists, and collaborators with the Germans. At the same time, the Australian government wanted the newly arrived refugees to become 'Australianised' as quickly as possible. But this policy was never matched by the resources required for successful assimilation. Classes for learning English were scarce and the migrant welfare agencies that did exist were mostly sponsored by private charities.

Now that the policy of multiculturalism has replaced assimilation, it is difficult for us to imagine how hard things really were for most of the immigrants who came to Australia in the immediate post-war decades. But an understanding of the history of their hardship is essential if we are to understand adequately the nature of our contemporary social relations. Australia of the late twentieth century is an Australia constituted by the struggles of the succeeding generations of immigrants and refugees.

It is crucial to note, however, that there is nothing uniform about the struggles of the post-war refugees. The experience of Australia that the various groups have had, has varied markedly. Each individual refugee has experienced Australia in a profoundly unique and contradictory manner. Each has been shaped by the Australia now past and has in turn shaped the Australia we live in today. Australia has been a site where people of many different backgrounds have had the opportunity to contribute in their own way to the formation of a truly multicultural society.

There are many, many stories to be told about the immigrants who have come to these shores. Some of these stories can be found in sociology books, but somehow it is only in the fictional form that these stories come alive, revealing their complexities. And so it is with Balodis's play, *Too Young for Ghosts*. The play reveals how the migration experience affected the social relationships of a group of people, but the broader theme it explores concerns the human spirit and how it can triumph over adversity.

Fazal Rizvi
Deakin University 1991

Above: Craig Ashley as McQuaide, Michael Winchester as Otto, Ivor Kants as Edvards. Sydney Theatre Company production 1985. Photo: Andrew Southam.Below: Josephine Byrnes as Ruth, Beverley Evans as Ilsa, Harriet Spalding as Lydia in the NIDA production 1989. Photo: Marco Bok.

Denis Moore as Edvards in the Melbourne Theatre Company production. 1985. Photo: David Parker.

Producing the Play

Working on this fascinating and challenging play was one of the most rewarding experiences of my professional life. The play presents great challenges and, therefore, opportunities to its director, designer and actors. It would be easy to get wrong.

During an extensive casting period, it became clear that those who read the play fell almost immediately into two camps and the ultimate response from the reviewers was similar. There were those who found the parallel plots and the complex time structure frustrating. They thought it undermined the comparatively simple and moving story of the group of Latvian immigrants. Even at the workshop at the Playwrights' Conference there had been those arguing for the removal of the Leichhardt scenes. There was another group, however, who were excited by these complexities and felt that the parallels and reverberations gave the play stature. They were undoubtedly right and we made sure we chose the cast from this group.

The practical challenges of the play are fascinating. From the outset it was clear to the designer Eamon Darcy and myself that we must find a simple solution to the design needs and the various character changes (sometimes within a speech!). Anyone who tries to produce the piece with elaborate sets and complicated costume changes is doomed to failure.

Eamon and I discussed a conventional raked stage but ultimately hit on the device of a rake 'in reverse', thus exploiting the Arts Centre Studio's steeply raked seating and arena stage. The highest point was the front corner and the sense of distance that was therefore achieved in a relatively small space worked well, especially for the Leichhardt and canefields scenes. Eamon painted the floor with an abstract design, almost suggesting an aerial photograph of

Australia's interior. A scrim surround (behind which the actors could be seen approaching), and a corrugated iron 'cyc' which assisted the lighting designer Jamie Lewis in providing wonderful glaring brightness for many of the Australian scenes, completed the set.

The only piece of furniture was a bed which popped out of the floor (at its highest point) for the childbirth scene. It was a thematically correct decision, but in practice, and in retrospect, it was a mistake. The simplicity of the design and the production meant that when the bed appeared it was a distraction.

The changes of character were achieved with great simplicity. Simple non-specific but evocative costumes were worn and minor changes (like the adding of a hat, or glasses or a different physicality) indicated the necessary changes. As the play progressed these became even simpler.

The task set by the play (and Eamon's sparse design) was to find an acting style that somehow matched the extraordinary power of the writing. Everyday naturalism didn't (and won't) work, and generalised emotion was to be avoided. We searched for a rigorous simplicity and rigorous use of the words. A superficial examination of Janis's work can suggest coldness (and he has been accused of such by some reviewers). Nothing could be further from the truth. His writing is passionate and full of (sometimes suppressed) emotion. But it is uncompromisingly unsentimental and that is what we sought to capture.

The play opened to mixed reviews. Some of the reviewers thought the piece too complex and feared that it would not be understood by the audience. Some theatre people thought likewise and came backstage at the previews shaking their heads and worrying about its 'obscurity'.In fact, the audiences in a television age in which great imaginative leaps are often demanded of them, had no trouble following it and generally found the play to be a moving and profound experience. I still meet people who say it was one of the most satisfying evenings they have experienced in the theatre. It clearly has the potential to be just that, and more. Sitting in the audience and watching the end of the play as Ilse gently sings to her new-born Australian baby (which we all romantically believed was really Janis himself) was an overwhelmingly moving experience. This moment somehow captures the essence of what the play is about and speaks to us so profoundly about the post-war Australian experience.

Now the play has the full recognition it deserves. It is an important play. Janis is writing two others, following the journey of the same characters and their children up to the present day. The resulting trilogy is certain to be one of our most important theatrical statements about ourselves.

Roger Hodgman
Melbourne Theatre Company, 1991

Too Young for Ghosts was first commissioned by the Sydney Theatre Company under the Dead Authors Subsidise the Living Scheme and was later workshopped at the 1984 Australian National Playwrights Conference, directed by Terence Clarke. The play was first performed by the Melbourne Theatre Company at the Studio, Victorian Arts Centre, on 4 July 1985 with the following cast:

ISLE	Pamela Rabe
RUTH	Mary Sitarenos
LYDIA/ANGIE	Robynne Bourne
KARL	Brandon Burke
OTTO	Geoff Revell
EDVARDS/LEICHHARDT	Denis Moore
LEONIDS/GILBERT	John O'May
MURPHY/G.I. SAM/BOURKE	Bill Fox
PHILLIPS/G.I. JOE McQUAIDE	Robert Essex

Designed by Eamon D'arcy
Lighting Design by Jamie Lewis
Directed by Roger Hodgman

CHARACTERS

ILSE, aged twenty-eight
RUTH, thirty-two
LYDIA/ANGIE, aged twenty-five and thirty-five
KARL, twenty-two
OTTO, twenty-six
EDVARDS/LEICHHARDT, thirty-four
LEONIDS/GILBERT, thirty-two
MURPHY/G.I. SAM/BOURKE, sixteen and twenty-three
PHILLIPS/G.I JOE/McQUAIDE, forty-five

The doubling of characters is intentional and integral to the structure and meaning of the play.

SETTING

The action of the play takes places in North Queensland locations in 1845 and 1948-49; and in Stuttgart in 1947.

AUTHOR'S NOTE

There are fairly rapid switches in time and location and it is important that the design should facilitate this movement and not hamper the flow of action from scene to scene with unnecessary blackouts or set devices. The minimalist approach to setting and acting style is both necessary and desirable. Costume design is probably the most critical problem. The actors are not given time for elaborate changes so one costume must serve for different periods, characters and locations. The solution most likely lies in the way the action is framed: Leichhardt's journey and the D.P.s' time in Stuttgart are like a 'dreaming' experienced by the D.P.s in Australia in 1948-49. This leads to the entertainment of the idea of Leichhardt exploring Australia in a 1940s suit, or the whole cast wearing a uniform garb. The style of speech is also important. When the D.P.s talk amongst themselves they speak fluently and without accent. When they try to speak English to others their speech is accented and halting.

PROLOGUE

The displaced persons in silhouette sing:

BLOW BREEZE
(*Put Vejini*)

Blow breeze, set sail,
Blow breeze, set sail.
We are leaving our home
For a new land.

Blow breeze, set sail,
Blow breeze, set sail.
The past is the past,
A new beginning.

PART ONE

SCENE ONE

North Queensland, 1948. Cane barracks, night.
BOURKE *enters carrying a lantern. He is followed by* KARL, ILSE, EDVARDS, RUTH, LYDIA, OTTO *and* LEONIDS. ILSE *wears a Latvian shawl.*

BOURKE: Well, this is it. Your new home, such as it is. Come the morning the Cane Growers will be thinking what to do with you. They were reckoning on one married couple to a gang of single blokes; the woman to do the cookin'. You'll be finding a wood-burning stove through there; bit hot in summer, but warms up like a biscuit tin in winter. Mind you, it's not a scheme I fancy meself, one woman to half a dozen blokes. God never intended it.
KARL: There's only two beds.
LYDIA: There's seven of us.
ILSE: It's worse than the ship.
RUTH: We'll have to sleep in shifts.
OTTO: There must be more.
LEONIDS: Turn on the light.
EDVARDS: No electricity. No bulbs.
BOURKE: Thought you buggers was s'posed to talk English. No use makin' you gangers if you don't. How's a man to tell you what to do? You speak English, or not?
KARL: Yes. I talk.

[*Pause.*]

BOURKE: That was it, eh? Not much to be goin' on with. You'll have to learn the language or me kids'll be throwin' stones at you and callin' you for all sorts of spies and wogs. Mind you, you'll confuse them for a while, not bein' Ities or Greeks.

[ILSE *knocks on the wall. Some jump.*]

ILSE: Feel the walls. All iron. Tiny room, iron walls, iron roof, iron stove, like an oven.
BOURKE: Admiring the architecture, eh? Not bad, is it? Galvanised iron. The all-purpose building material, put

up a house in a week. What more does a man need? Just talk amongst yourselves, I can talk to meself all night.

[*Pause.*]

ILSE: What do we do for food? He's the land owner. Do we have to buy from him? Go on, ask him.

KARL: I don't know. What are the words? [*To* BOURKE, *miming, putting his fingers to his mouth and speaking with an accent*] Ead! Ead!

BOURKE: You mean eat. Eat. You just had tea. There was even baked beans left in the tin. [*Suspiciously*] You're not suggestin' I'm a mean man?

KARL: [*waving his hand to stop him*] I show. [*Trying to take* BOURKE's *lantern*] I buy.

BOURKE: Bugger off. You got a couple of bloody lanterns of your own. I'm not walkin' home in the dark.

LEONIDS: Show him some money.

[*The D.P.s check their pockets.*]

BOURKE: Bit over ten bob, eh? You're rich. You'll soon be making a quid if you bend your backs. Cane cutting is a cream of a job.

KARL: [*offering the money and trying to take the lantern*] I buy. Eat.

BOURKE: [*refusing to hand over the lantern*] I told you once. Not much of a feed in it and you wouldn't want to drink the kero.

ILSE: He's stupid. [*Coming between them*] Me.

BOURKE: [*laughing*] If you give me a shilling and your missus, you can surely have the lantern.

[*He takes the shilling then gives* KARL *the lantern.*]

KARL: [*crowing*] You see. He understands.

BOURKE: [*winking at* ILSE] Couldn't ask for a fairer bargain.

RUTH: You just swapped Ilse for a lantern.

ILSE: Old habits die hard.

[*They laugh.*]

EDVARDS: O.K. That's a fine piece of financial wizardry.

[ILSE *gives the lantern back to* BOURKE *and takes the shilling.*]

BOURKE: No deal, eh? Too bad.

[ILSE *mimes falling asleep, waking and preparing breakfast.*]

ILSE: Food.

BOURKE: Aha! Now I see. Breakfast. There's a box of stuff on the table. Bread, jam, eggs, tea.

ILSE: How much is?

BOURKE: [*speaking with an accent*] You keep. Pay later. Tomorrow. Domani. Shit! Now you've got me doin' it. Bedtime. [*Miming*] Sleep. OK. Couple of you stay here, the rest follow me. OK.

[*He starts to go. The D.P.s look confused.*]

EDVARDS: OK.

BOURKE: Thank God someone speaks the lingo.

EDVARDS: I think he wants us to follow him.

[*They all pick up their bags.*]

BOURKE: Na, na, na, nah! Not all of you. [*Separating* KARL *and* ILSE *from the others*] You two [*speaking with an accent*] stay here. Good night.

ILSE: Good night.

KARL: [*shaking* BOURKE'*s hand*] Good night.

[*Much to* BOURKE'*s discomfort* ILSE *shakes his hand.*]

ILSE: Good night.

BOURKE: Good night. The rest of you come with me.

LYDIA: Where's he taking us?

EDVARDS: Don't worry. O.K. There's only one of him, he has no gun and it's too warm for Siberia.

LEONIDS: Edvards is full of joy as ever.

[LYDIA *cries. They follow the disappearing* BOURKE. ILSE *and* KARL *are left.*]

ILSE: [*Quietly*] This is our new home.

SCENE TWO

North Queensland, 1845. The explorers' camp. Day. LEICHHARDT *takes a bearing with a sextant. He wears a coolie's hat.* MURPHY *stands beside him with a book, pen and ink.* LEICHHARDT *reads the sextant, hands it to* MURPHY *and prepares to write. He checks the previous entry.* LEICHHARDT *speaks with a German accent. In the camp,* GILBERT *crushes some leaves and bark which he puts in a billy.*

LEICHHARDT: Ach! What is this?

[*Re-reading the sextant*] You have not fiddled this?

MURPHY: No, sir, Doctor Leichhardt.

LEICHHARDT: Then something is not right or we have gone backwards from yesterday. Impossible, no? With the sun over the same shoulder, it is so easy to say north, south, east and west But north from where, or east to where, that is a little more difficult. Ja?

MURPHY: [*hopefully*] Can't you take another reading?

LEICHHARDT: Not today. We know we are here so we cannot be lost.

MURPHY: Yeah, but where is here?

LEICHHARDT: We will see tomorrow.

[LEICHHARDT *takes the book, pen and ink and goes up to the camp.* MURPHY *tries to read the sextant.*]

GILBERT: This morning as we crested that ridge, I thought I could smell the sea on the breeze. From the north-west.

LEICHHARDT: Sometimes I think I can smell my mother's back garden and fresh bread baking in the oven. But that is in Austria and my mother has been dead for some years.

GILBERT: I am suggesting we could be nearer to the Gulf than you think.

LEICHHARDT: In Austria we have a saying, 'Take your eyes in your hand and your nose will show you.' You think we should follow your nose? [GILBERT *says nothing*] Quite so.

[*taking an axe and going off singing into the trees*]

Don't ask me, friend, why I rushed away
And left you with a heart that's full of pain.
Don't ask me why, why I said, 'I love you',
That's one thing now that I can't understand.

[*There is the sound of chopping, off.*]

MURPHY: [*showing* GILBERT *the sextant*] Can you read where we are, Mr Gilbert?

GILBERT: No, Johnny.

MURPHY: We're truly lost, then.

GILBERT: There's a line of marked trees all the way back to the Darling Downs waiting to be joined up like dots in a child's drawing.

MURPHY: It's a big country–bigger'an I can think–but I seen a lot of it in the past eight months. An' I'd like to see a whole lot more, so dyin' in the middle of nowhere ain't part of me plans. If we was to go home now, I'd be goin' home a man.

[*There is the sharp crack of a branch breaking.* MURPHY *jumps for his gun.*]

Halt. Who goes there?

PHILLIPS: [*off*] The Queen of Sheba, who yer bloody think? Put that gun down, you feeble-minded idiot afore you shoot someone.

[PHILLIPS *enters.*]

MURPHY: Sorry, Phillips.

PHILLIPS: Yer more damn skittish than an unbroken filly. Where's the gallant leader?

GILBERT: Carving his inspirational message into yet another tree.

PHILLIPS: 'L eighteen forty five'? Wonder who he reckons will be readin' 'em after we're gone. Last year it was 'L eighteen forty four', next year it'll be L eighteen forty six.

GILBERT: That's progress. What's the big hurry?

PHILLIPS: Blacks' camp, Mr Gilbert, about a mile away. Could mean nosh. He'll be wantin' to know.

GILBERT: If you want to be sure of a fair share you better be getting there before Doctor Leichhardt. You go too, Johnny.

MURPHY: Ain't you comin', Mr Gilbert.

GILBERT: I've work to do. I'll stay and inform the good doctor when he's done attackin' that tree.

PHILLIPS: Com'n, boyo, me arse is eatin' me trousers.

MURPHY: I'll bring some back for you, Mr Gilbert.

GILBERT: Thank you, Johnny.

[MURPHY *and* PHILLIPS *go.*]

PHILLIPS: Mind where you're pointin' that damn thing.

[RUTH *enters opposite* GILBERT. *She stops and looks briefly, then turns to go.* GILBERT *turns in time to see her leaving. He stares.* LEICHHARDT *comes down into the camp. He carries the axe and mops his brow. He drinks from the billy.*]

LEICHHARDT: Good tea. Like consommé. Probably quite medicinal. [*He spits out some leaves and drinks some more.*]

GILBERT: Yes. Should be good for the bowels. It was a tanning mixture for my bird skins.

LEICHHARDT: Delicious! You must make some more. It will help sustain us on the road ahead.

GILBERT: Just now I thought I saw someone.

LEICHHARDT: Yes. It is me.

GILBERT: No. Before.

LEICHHARDT: So. Who was it?

GILBERT: I didn't see.

LEICHHARDT: [*gloating*] Who did you think you saw when you didn't see?

[*Pause.*]

It is your language.

[*He laughs.*]

GILBERT: Perhaps it was a native.

LEICHHARDT: Perhaps you are seeing viney-viney like the blacks.

GILBERT: We are the viney-viney to the blacks. I think they are right in believing that spirits roam this land.

LEICHHARDT: Perhaps you could collect them instead of birds. Spirit is lighter. The rate you are collecting, my trees will be devoided of life and your boxes will break the backs of the oxen before we reach Port Essington.

GILBERT: If we reach there.

LEICHHARDT: I will. Even if it kills me.

[*He laughs and drains the billy.*]

Excellent brew, Mr Gilbert.

[*Cooees are heard off.*]

KARL: [*off*] Hello!

GILBERT: It's the others. They found a native's camp.

LEICHHARDT: Ah ha! You see! Just like the promised land, food lying on the ground.

GILBERT: Hardly manna from heaven.

LEICHHARDT: Depends on how you look. I will go see.

GILBERT: About a mile that way.

[*Hardly bothering to look,* LEICHHARDT *goes.*]

LEICHHARDT: Ja. Ja. My nose will show me.

[GILBERT *is left in the camp alone.*]

SCENE THREE

The refugee camp, Stuttgart, 1947.

KARL *enters carrying a large battered suitcase. He wears a cheap suit.*

KARL: [*calling*] Hello! Hey! Anyone home? For God's sake, Edvards, come on. I don't want you to get lost after all this time.

[EDVARDS *enters carrying a wooden box of young chickens. He is dressed in standard refugee attire. American army uniforms dyed blue. His gait is awkward and one side of his face is scarred.*]

EDVARDS: Okay. Okay. What do I do with these birds?

KARL: Put them down for a minute.

EDVARDS: You sure this is the right place?

KARL: It should be. I don't understand why there's no one about. Maybe they've been moved to another barracks.

EDVARDS: Can't we just leave this stuff here?

KARL: No, Stuttgart is crawling with thieves. All this is my livelihood, my future. I worked in the Yanks' Quartermaster Store before they put me away. And I made a lot of contacts so I could set myself up in business. What I haven't got I can get, for a price. You name it.

EDVARDS: How about a bottle of booze?

KARL: Later, after we've tracked down the others.

EDVARDS: Maybe they emigrated while you were in gaol.

KARL: I fell in with a good bunch. They would have let me know.

EDVARDS: You go, okay? I'll wait and keep watch over your precious future. [KARL *puts his case down.*]

KARL: They can't be far away. What a lucky thing you bumped into me. I didn't believe my eyes. What a double-barrel surprise we've got for them.

EDVARDS: The self-made man and the man-made man.

KARL: Here, have a cigarette. Lucky Strikes, the best. You'll be fine.

EDVARDS: I'm a dumb ox some clown assembled in a butcher's shop for a joke. Who would believe a man was made of so many pieces? OK? After seeing corpses by the trainload, I'm not sure they're all mine. An arm off this one, leg off that one.

KARL: Dr Frankenstein did a good job on you. You look all in one piece now.

[*We hear the distant sound of people singing.*]

EDVARDS: OK. Some comfort.

KARL: Ssh! Come here and listen. Someone's coming.

[*The singing increases in volume as the singers approach.*]

DON'T ASK ME, FRIEND
(*Draugs ne Jauta*)

Don't ask me, friend, why I rushed away
And left you with a heart that's full of pain.
Don't ask me why, why I said I loved you,
That's one thing now that I can't under-
stand.
Don't ask me why, why I said I loved you.
That's one thing now that I can't understand.
Could it have been the madness of
springtime,
That set our hearts alight with burning love?
But autumn's wind has chilled my deep
desire,
Don't ask me how, I'll never really know.

But autumn's wind has chilled my deep desire,
Don't ask me how, I'll never really know.

[*After hearing a few lines of the song,* EDVARDS *stamps out his cigarette.*]

KARL: Hey, you didn't smoke that. They're American, hard to get. [*Picking it up*] That's the profit margin on a pack.

EDVARDS: [*agitatedly*] OK. OK. I need a drink. No. Better I don't stay.

KARL: Take another cigarette. There's plenty. You can't go now. You were given up for dead and here you are. A miracle.

EDVARDS: A mistake.

KARL: Wait and see Ruth. She never believed you were dead and she's been faithful. You want a beautiful woman like that to become a nun? Who would believe I'd seen you if you slip through my fingers like a ghost?

EDVARDS: OK. But I should be given her some warning.

[KARL *steers* EDVARDS *into the room and leaves him with the case and the chickens.*]

KARL: You leave that to me.

EDVARDS: Tell her first what to expect. OK?

KARL: Relax. It mightn't even be her. You're worse than a bridegroom. Wait [KARL *goes out into the barrack square/clearing and joins in the singing. While* KARL *sings,* OTTO *comes on stage ahead of the others.*]

OTTO: [*calling the others, off*] Hurry. It is Karl.

[LYDIA, RUTH, LEONIDS *and* ILSE *enter.*]

What'd I tell you? Only one person sings like that. Karlo Caruso.

[*Shaking* KARL'*s hand*] Look at that suit, for God's sake.

KARL: You've put on weight, Otto.

OTTO: It's that cow fodder they feed us. Spinach and oats. I'll be giving milk next.

[*The greetings are polite and restrained.*]

KARL: Lydia.

LYDIA: Hello, Karl. They let you out early?

KARL: Two months off for good behaviour.

RUTH: Good behaviour, lover boy?

KARL: You know me. You look a million dollars. Wait till you see what a surprise I've got for you. You'll be forever in my debt.

RUTH: [*laughing*] The big shot is back all right.

OTTO: Where did you get that suit?

LEONIDS: It's how they dress in American gaols. The gangsters, anyway. We've all seen the films. [*To* KARL] Ruth has told me all about you.

[RUTH *takes* LEONIDS' *arm.*]

RUTH: Karl, meet Leonids.

[KARL *shakes* LEONIDS' *hand.*]

We're getting married.

KARL: Oh, well ... you mean – but – what the hell.

ILSE: Have I become invisible?

[KARL *goes to her and swings her round.*]

KARL: Four months of dreams in the lock-up when not once did you come and see me. Give me a kiss to prove you're real.

[KARL *tries to kiss her. She laughs and pulls away.*]

ILSE: You got yourself in there. Why should I worry?

KARL: Didn't you even miss me? I missed you.

ILSE: You're such a boy.

KARL: [*saving face*] A boy. How do you like that? Have a Lucky Strike.

OTTO: American tobacco. Seventh heaven.

[*Two G.I.s cross upstage. They look as though they have just come off the battlefield; as tattered and worn as the explorers.* G.I. JOE *whistles.*]

G.I. SAM: Hi, girls! How's about throwin' over those losers and showin' us a good time?

KARL: [*waving and speaking with an accent*] Hi, Joes.

G.I. JOE: I'm Joe, he's Sam and you gotta be the ugliest broad I ever seen. We was addressin' ourselves to the ones with the bumps on the front. *Comprendy?*

ILSE: They murdered Elmer Karklins.

KARL: Ssh!

ILSE: They understand nothing.

G.I. JOE: Ah! See ya later, girls.

KARL: See yous, Joes. It doesn't hurt to be polite.

RUTH: They're just a couple of unknown soldiers.

KARL: Unknown soldiers?

ILSE: Was there ever a soldier who gave a woman his right name?

[*The women laugh.*]

KARL: They murdered Elmer?

LEONIDS: Shot. Not by those two.

OTTO: When you were put away, Elmer took over your still. His last brew killed one man, blinded five and put a dozen in hospital. The Yank provos were taking him to gaol for manslaughter, but Elmer must've thought they'd hand him over to the Russians. That's how his brain worked, probably from drinking his own brew.

LYDIA: Otto.

ILSE: He ran and they shot him. Just like at the cinema. What happens to all crooks.

KARL: Silly bugger. The Yanks are good Joes.

RUTH: Elmer wasn't so bad.

ILSE: If you didn't drink.

[OTTO *produces a flask.*]

OTTO: Want to try his brew?

KARL: No thanks.

[OTTO *drinks.*]

LYDIA: Where'd you get that? Have you gone mad?

OTTO: It's one of his earlier brews. Not bad, but not as good as Karl's. [*To* KARL] Try it.

KARL: Well, if you say it s OK.

[OTTO *misses handing the flask to* KARL *and gropes about.*]

OTTO: Now where did he go? Karl? Anyone? I know you're all hiding.

[*The others laugh.*]

LYDIA: You're not funny, Otto.

RUTH: Before you all get blind drunk I want my little surprise.

KARL: Oh, well, yes, look. Give me a minute to set it up. Wait till I call you.

[KARL *goes into the room.*]

EDVARDS: OK. Is it Ruth?

KARL: In a minute she'll be coming through the door.

EDVARDS: Did you tell her?

KARL: There's been a slight hitch.

EDVARDS: OK. I'll give you more time.

[He starts to go.]

KARL: Look, it's not so easy to–

EDVARDS: The waiting is also hard. OK. Send her out to me. Then I'll know you told her.

[He goes.]

KARL: For God's sake come back.

RUTH: *[leading the others into the room]* Coming ready or not. Well, whatever it is, it doesn't exactly hit you in the face.

OTTO: Perhaps we're supposed to search for it.

KARL: Chickens. A box full of chickens. A surprise for everyone.

RUTH: I expected something more exotic.

ILSE: *[laughing]* A peacock at least.

KARL: The idea is you raise them till they're big enough to eat.

LYDIA: Someone else can have mine. I could never cold-bloodedly choose one to die ... ugh.

LEONIDS: They'll do it for you. When they sort out the pecking order you take the weakest, kill it and eat it.

LYDIA: Horrible creatures.

RUTH: What sort of man would surprise a woman with a batch of chickens?

KARL: A businessman. A farmer in gaol gave me some contacts in the chicken business.

RUTH: What's in the case?

KARL: *[opening it]* I'm glad you asked. My shop. Underwear, tinned food, cigarettes, chocolates, everything is for sale. *[Taking out a bottle and some glasses for the women]* And some of my own vintage liquor I salted away. Four months old.

OTTO: You have to hand it to Karl. He goes to gaol, a small-time bootlegger, and he comes back a big-time businessman in a suit. I should be so lucky.

KARL: *[pouring drinks]* Where's the luck? I went to gaol to make the contacts. And the suit I paid for with a gold tooth.

LYDIA: Since when did you have gold teeth?

KARL: A year ago the ground was littered with teeth.

OTTO: You mean you pulled teeth from corpses?

KARL: It's easier. A live man will bite you. The dead have no use for teeth. They don't eat the worms, the worms eat them.

[*He laughs.*]

Try some of this, it'll take the bad taste out of your mouth.

[*They drink.*]

I'm back in business, so if there's anything you fancy to make life bearable while you're here ...

LYDIA: We won't be here long so you can sell those horrid chickens. By the time they're big enough to eat, we'll be in Australia, thank God.

KARL: Australia?

OTTO: Yes. We're all going to Australia.

KARL: Who? All of who?

LEONIDS: Us here. Nothing's definite yet.

KARL: Why not America? Why not stay here? Australia?

RUTH: He's getting used to the idea.

LEONIDS: We've waited here two years for the Yanks to liberate our homes from the Russians. Why should they bother? We fought for the Germans. If we stick around here we'll probably end up in Siberia. Australia's a safe place to go and do a bit of honest work.

KARL: I have work here. For the first time since the war I can see how to make myself a bit of money. What's there? Light so bright you go blind.

ILSE: The same thing happens here from drinking bad booze.

KARL: Are you going?

ILSE: If they'll have me. They're asking for single women, so they must have work for us.

KARL: Single women, eh? Doesn't that make you wonder?

OTTO: They're only taking singles, men and women, but we'll pull a swifty by getting married when we get there.

LYDIA: A double wedding. Me and Otto, Ruth and Leonids. We don't mind making it a triple with you and Ilse.

KARL: What about Edvards?

RUTH: I've accepted he's dead, and I'm a widow. I won't regret leaving. [RUTH *and* LEONIDS *embrace.*]

KARL: Oh, well ... Look, if you're so keen to be going to the jungles, you better look through my stock. You're sure to find some little luxury to make the journey more pleasant.

[KARL *takes* ILSE *aside as the others look in this case.*]

KARL: I need you to do something for me. But first I have a surprise for you. Close your eyes.

ILSE: You're going to try to kiss me again.

KARL: Why not?

ILSE: I'm half a dozen years older than you.

KARL: I like older women.

ILSE: Yet you treat me like a little girl.

KARL: It's the only way I can stop you treating me like a son. Come on. Close your eyes.

[*She does.* KARL *unfurls a Latvian shawl and drapes it over her shoulders.*]

LYDIA: Oh, Ilse. A shawl from Latvia.

RUTH: So beautiful.

OTTO: [*whistling*] That must have cost a whole mouthful of teeth.

KARL: You can open your eyes now.

LYDIA: Men understand nothing. You always want to look. She can feel it on her skin.

OTTO: It must be pinching her. She's crying.

KARL: It's just a gift, Ilse. Open your eyes, for God's sake.

ILSE: Oh, Karl.

RUTH: At least say thank you. I'll swap you any day. You can't wear a couple of chickens to a ball.

OTTO: No. A modest woman would need at least three.

LEONIDS: It's too beautiful to belong here–like sunshine in a nightmare. [*The light changes.*]

SCENE FOUR

North Queensland, 1948. The cane barracks. Night.

ILSE: [*quietly*] This is our new home. Our ducks and chickens lived in more comfort. I thought these people came from Europe with knowledge that was hundreds of years old. There's no evidence of it. Perhaps we've fallen amongst exiles who have been sent as far from civilisation as possible. Is this the best they can do in a hundred and fifty years? They live as if they don't expect to stay.

KARL: I certainly don't. And while they're busy making up their minds, I can make a bit of money. When they don't know what they want, they can be sold anything. All I have to do is feel out the market.

ILSE: Does everyone who comes here have to start from scratch? There must have been some border crossing where knowledge and memories were wiped out. I escaped the treatment and remember too much.

KARL: We only have to stay till our contract is up. Latvia could be free by then and we'll go home and reclaim my father's farm.

ILSE: I don't believe for a moment I'll ever see Latvia again.

KARL: That's my only dream. I made a mistake coming here. A big mistake.

ILSE: Are you sorry you married me after only three weeks?

KARL: What a wedding, not even time to knock up a batch of grog. And I would've liked a proper photograph, just the two of us, instead of a piece of newspaper. I can't send this to my mother.

ILSE: We can buy a camera and have some real photos taken.

KARL: At least I made the papers. New Australians marry in triple wedding. We look confused, like smiling dummies, as if we didn't know what we were getting into. Too true.

ILSE: Why did you ask me to marry you?

KARL: Why did you say yes?

[*Pause.*]

ILSE: Two lost people together stand a better chance than one adrift.

KARL: A nice proposition.

ILSE: You shouldn't have asked.

KARL: You could have refused. You did last time.

ILSE: Circumstances have changed. Besides, I got the best of the deal. I know what I'm letting myself in for.

KARL: What's that?

ILSE: Knowing you can't be relied on. That's the one certainty in my life. A bad risk guards against complacency and seems a good way to deal with a strange country.

KARL: You really know how to make a man feel good.

ILSE: You got more than you bargained for. You were looking for a mother, I gave you a wife. I can comfort you if you like, the way a mother would.

KARL: No, keep away.

ILSE: Wives are harder to get rid of, especially when they give themselves so cheaply.

KARL: Not to me, you didn't. I'll be paying the rest of my life. I don't know what the hell I had to smile about in that photograph.

ILSE: I was squeezing your bum, remember?

[RUTH *enters.*]

We were just looking at the wedding photographs and remembering what fun it was.

RUTH: It's different for you. For me it wasn't real.

ILSE: Karl wishes it wasn't.

KARL: Where are you sleeping?

RUTH: With Edvards. In another iron shed just like this one, no better, no worse.

KARL: I'll go and take a look.

ILSE: He has to mark out his territory, like a tom-cat.

[KARL *goes.*]

RUTH: In the dark these places look awful and feel cold. Yet the iron sweats. Perhaps everything will look better in the morning.

[*Pause.*]

Are you fighting already?

ILSE: Still.

RUTH: I didn't think it possible to share a bed with a man and not touch him. Even when you're asleep something watchful comes between you. Edvards doesn't seem to notice. One side of him feels nothing any more and in the other the nerves are twisted. All messages get confused. I lie there awake.

ILSE: What will you do about Leonids?

RUTH: Oh, Ilse, I'm so alone. When the train brought us here, stopping in the night in the middle of nowhere, I waited for the guard to come and put me off, beside the train, alone, with nothing. A worthless woman. The way the Russians put grandmothers off beside the track and saved themselves a bullet. And then the train would move off, and in the window, Leonids would be watching me as if I was a knife in his side.

ILSE: Tell him to go away.

RUTH: I'm going with him.

ILSE: Where to?

RUTH: We'll take the train and get off somewhere together, when we have enough money saved. Two people should be able to disappear in a country this size.

[LEONIDS *enters with his suitcase.*]

LEONIDS: This seems to be where the extra bed is.

ILSE: I suppose that's where you'll have to sleep.

LEONIDS: Just for tonight.

[RUTH *holds out her hand to* LEONIDS.]

There's another room, but it's full of fertiliser. Blood and bone. We'll clean it out tomorrow.

[RUTH *and* LEONIDS *embrace.*]

ILSE: I'll leave you alone for a moment.

[KARL *enters.*]

KARL: [*to* LEONIDS] Oh, you're here. Thought we'd lost you.

[*The light changes.*]

SCENE FIVE

Stuttgart, 1947.

EDVARDS: Ruthie?

OTTO: Someone's out there.

EDVARDS: Ruth.

KARL: [*in reply to* RUTH'*s look*] Yes, it's Edvards. But wait a ...

[EDVARDS *walks away as* RUTH *goes out to him.* OTTO, LYDIA *and* ILSE *go to look.* LEONIDS *and* KARL *stay in the room.*]

OTTO: Guess who's back from the dead?

RUTH: Edvards.

EDVARDS: Don't look, Ruthie.

[*She comes round to him. He covers her eyes.*]

Don't look. OK?

LEONIDS: You should have told her straight away.

KARL: I tried ... I was going to ... She was all over you. What was I to say in front of everyone: 'Let that man go. Your husband has come back from the dead with only half his face?

LEONIDS: That should be me. [*Going out to the others*] That would be easier.

[RUTH *moves* EDVARDS' *hand away and gently touches his face.*]

EDVARDS: It doesn't hurt, not to touch. OK. You are more beautiful than ever, while I have been made by man, almost in his image.

RUTH: Don't talk like that.

[EDVARDS *turns to the others.*]

EDVARDS: Are these your friends?

[LYDIA *can't look at him.*]

RUTH: Yes. Lydia and Otto.

OTTO: I'm glad you pulled through. I always wanted to meet a real hero.

EDVARDS: You've got the horse by the dirty end, my friend. Heroes look like Karl. OK?

RUTH: This is Ilse, and Leonids.

ILSE: Hello, Edvards.

[ILSE *kisses his cheek and then takes* RUTH'*s hand.*]

LEONIDS: Pleased to meet you.

EDVARDS: [*to all of them*] Take a good look and don't pity me. Better yet, think of me as Janus the two-headed god. One face looks forward, one face looks back. Which is which? That is the riddle. It is not as you'd expect. This one [*his good side*] is my past. And this is my future. It doesn't look so good.

[EDVARDS *laughs. The others relax.* KARL *joins them.*]

OTTO: It's not so damn good for anyone.

EDVARDS: OK. Here we all are, two years after the war, still in the uniforms of the victors. A displaced people. No past and no future. In that respect I am luckier than you.

LYDIA: Your future is no more stamped in your face than ours is and it doesn't mean we'll spend the rest of our lives with a jackboot on our necks.

EDVARDS: We are a problem. OK. No one knows what to do with us, but the Russians would find a solution, like the Germans with the Jews.

[*He laughs.*]

OK. Look at you all. Waiting to be saved.

LYDIA: You do what you like. Otto and I are going to Australia.

EDVARDS: Go. Away. Anywhere. OK? Karl, I need that drink. The funeral is over. Don't worry, I will pay. OK.

KARL: [*going*] No, no. It's all right. On the house.

OTTO: [*to* KARL] This bottle is empty.

LYDIA: You've had enough. I want to go.

EDVARDS: Bring enough for everybody and I won't take charity. I insist on paying.

[*He takes a dental plate from his mouth and crushes it under his heel.*]

LEONIDS: Jesus Christ, what are you doing?

OTTO: His false teeth. Gold ones.

[KARL *returns with a bottle.* EDVARDS *takes the bottle and gives* KARL *a tooth.*]

EDVARDS: That should put me in credit.

KARL: [*trying to return it*] I can't take that. Not out of your mouth. Pay me later. I know a dentist who can repair that.

EDVARDS: [*refusing*] It didn't fit right and anyway it gave me a false smile.

[*He drinks.*]

A man only needs teeth to tear meat from bones or to hold onto his lover. OK. Already I've noticed all the cats and dogs have been eaten and I'm a married man again.

[*He embraces* RUTH.]

KARL: Ruth, take these. See if you can get them fixed.

EDVARDS: No. OK. [*To* KARL] You want me to pay in cash? If I have to sell them on the black market, I won't get as good a price as you. You do me a favour by taking them.

KARL: It makes me feel like shit.

EDVARDS: A business man has no conscience. OK? And for the taste of shit there is an antidote. Let's get drunk. I have a lot to remember. [EDVARDS *puts his arm round* RUTH *and starts to go. All except* LEONIDS *follow.*]

SCENE SIX

North Queensland, 1845. Day.

GILBERT *dissects a bird and makes entries in his journal.* LEICHHARDT *enters carrying the carcass of an emaciated dingo.*

LEICHHARDT: I am back.

GILBERT: [*not looking up*] So I see. And smell. Where did you find that dog?

LEICHHARDT: Not find. I caught it on the path to the waterhole. It comes, panting, very slowly–

GILBERT: The maggots were carrying it off?

LEICHHARDT: I killed it with a stone.

GILBERT: Doesn't that nose of yours tell you it has an intolerably bad odour?

LEICHHARDT: Caused only by an insufficient diet.

GILBERT: Now that we're out of supplies, we must smell as rotten as that dog to the natives. No wonder they run off howling.

[*Pause.*] Have you given any thought to turning back?

LEICHHARDT: No!

GILBERT: My work on this expedition is finished. I have no blank pages left in my journal.

LEICHHARDT: Then you can no longer record my shortcomings.

GILBERT: I can no longer record my observations about my specimens.

LEICHHARDT: Good! I think you are sitting too long in the one place, looking into the gutses of chickens. Raise your head a little and look to the horizon. Have some vision, man, this country is more than one bush clearing and the next.

GILBERT: We merely see things differently and place different importance on what we see. You charge from one thing to another and because you cover a lot of ground you think you have seen a lot. Consequently, you make no sense of what you see or how one thing is related to another. You want to see it all and yet see nothing. Others will come afterwards and be astounded at the things we missed. But sit still a moment. Notice this tree grows in this soil, that this beetle is found on this tree and the bird feeds on its berries. Look deeper still. Open up the bird, split the tree, dig in the soil. That way you can steal nature's secrets. You can learn so much just sitting here. Move fifty yards in any direction and everything is different. My world is what is within my field of vision. If I go to see what is there, I miss what is here. I build a picture of this clearing by putting together the little things that make it up. I build a picture of Australia by putting together the clearings. I am happy, but for the knowledge that I won't see it all. I can't cover the ground fast enough.

LEICHHARDT: I'm for covering it as quickly as possible. The further the horizon the better.

GILBERT: So long as there's a tree you can head for.

LEICHHARDT: This is no ordinary adventure, Mr Gilbert. We are in a new land in a new time. You look and you see specimens and you see danger. You are not seeing the woods for the trees. I am discovering the way for your 'others' to follow and the trees I mark will stand as monuments to our achievements. Thousands will come from the stagnant civilisation of Europe where men kill each other for a pocketful of soil. They will come with knowledge that is hundreds of years old and cultivate this Eden. The future is all around, larger than life, innocent and without secrets. There are no ghosts in her closets.

GILBERT: Except for the natives and their whole host of spirits.

LEICHHARDT: Pah! Black men and their viney-viney. Thousands of years they have been here and who can tell? They have hardly marked the soil.

SCENE SEVEN

Stuttgart, 1947. Day.

KARL *and* ILSE *are walking together.* KARL *kisses* ILSE. *She draws away.*

KARL: I thought you would be glad to see me. I thought you were sweet on me.

ILSE: I did some thinking while you were away too.

KARL: And now a man can't even kiss you. Doesn't that shawl mean anything to you?

[*She gives it back to him.*]

ILSE: You don't have to pay this much for a whore.

KARL: What do you mean? Don't put words in my mouth. I didn't mean that.

[*He moves to her. She doesn't resist.*]

It's yours. Unconditional. I sat in my cell for four months just thinking of you.

ILSE: And tobacco and booze, black market deals and gold teeth. The only way I can fit in with such schemes is as a–

KARL: What the hell do you think of me? I like your company. It's natural. Blame God. Even Adam had his Eve.

ILSE: You'll have to play Eve because you've got the apple.

[KARL *returns the shawl to her.*]

KARL: Here, please take it.

ILSE: If I bite, what is it that I'm supposed to learn?

KARL: [*laughing*] You want me to say I love you?

ILSE: Talk is cheap. Other men have loved me, as they loved other women.

[G.I. JOE *and* G.I. SAM *enter.*]

G.I. JOE: She's still here with the jerk in the suit. Com'n, Sam. Don't go all shy on me now.

[*They approach.*]

KARL: Hi, Joes.

G.I. JOE: I'm Joe. He's Sam. How ya doin', Fritz? Nice suit. Must be doin' all right in the black market. [*To* ILSE] You c'n do better than a two bit punk. Com'n, Sam, trot your stuff. I wanta do this very polite like.

G.I. SAM: While the suit's here?

G.I. JOE: Sure. Do it. He's a nice guy. OK, Fritz?

KARL: OK, Joe.

G.I. SAM: [*nervously*] Hiya, Ilsa. This is Joe Hallaran. Joe, this here's Ilsa.

G.I. JOE: Thanks for nothin', kid. As an icebreaker you could use a bit more steel in your pecker. [*To* ILSE] Hello, Miss Ilsa. Sam here's been tellin' me a lot about you and I'm real happy to make your acquaintance. You're real pretty.

[G.I. JOE *holds out his hand.* ILSE *doesn't take it.*]

KARL: He wants to meet you.

ILSE: He wants a whore.

KARL: [*to* ILSE] All of a sudden you've got a one track mind. [*To all*] I think hers–

G.I. JOE: I get the picture, Fritz. She's shy. Look, why don't you two jerks give a man a bit of room?

[*He waves* KARL *and* SAM *a few paces away.*]

ILSE: [*to* KARL] Where are you going? He's the trespasser.

G.I. JOE: Now, Miss Ilsa, Don't get me wrong. I'm not a bad sort of Joe. I'd like to get acquainted. [*Offering a small bottle to her*] *Pour vous, ma'amselle.*

[ILSE *doesn't take it.*]

G.I. SAM: That's French, Joe.

G.I. JOE: So I came via Paree.

G.I. SAM: She ain't French, though.

G.I. JOE: It's the language of love, ain't it? *Parfum!*

[*Pause.*]

OK. So it's bloody American after-shave, but the German girls go wild for it.

KARL: [*to* ILSE] He wants you to have that American cologne.

ILSE: Ask him when the American Joes will chase Joe Stalin out of my home instead of signing a pact. The Yanks believe in one law and one justice for all. When the Yanks sit down with the Russians and make law, there's justice for no one. Horseshit!

KARL: I don't know how to ask that, luckily.

G.I. JOE: I think I made a breakthrough here. She said 'Joe' twice.

G.I. SAM: Probably callin' us arseholes.

G.I. JOE: [*to* KARL] Fritz? What *fraulein sprechen?*

KARL: She likes Americans plenty ...

ILSE: G.I. Joes

[*She spits.*]

Shit.

G.I. JOE: [*prodding* KARL] She don't like Americans, do she? Well, you can tell her to go fuck herself on a barb-wire fence and crawl back to Siberia. [*To* ILSE] You think we wanted to fight this bloody war? You got no sense of gratitude. A man could practically screw his way from the beaches of Normandy. This is the first time I come across this. Well, sister, I had my head in a lot of laps and I ain't accustomed to such treatment.

[*He forcibly kisses her. She bites him. He reels back as* G.I. SAM *and* KARL *step in.*]

She fuckin' bit me! Blood!

G.I. SAM: Come on, Joe.

KARL: [*placatingly*] Sorry, Joe. She OK. Sorry.

[G.I. JOE *struggles with* G.I. SAM.]

G.I. JOE: She OK! She's fuckin' crazy. She nearly took my lip off. Goddamn cannibal .

G.I. SAM: Could'a been your pecker.

G.I. JOE: You think that's funny. You think it's so goddamn funny? You set me up.

G.I. SAM: I swear I never, I swear. I weren't the only one she had. You ain't missing anythin'. She'd just lie there while you ploughed a paddock.

G.I. JOE: Yeah! How come I hit the land mine?

G.I. SAM: Come on. Leave her to the suit.

G.I. JOE: [*to* KARL] You better watch yourself, Fritz, or she'll have you for fuckin' breakfast. [*To* ILSE] Bitch.

[*They go.*]

KARL: What the hell did you have to do that for? He was just being friendly.

ILSE: They think any woman is theirs for the taking. The spoils to the victors. Why didn't you stop him?

KARL: I thought you knew them. That Sam knew you.

ILSE: That's one cock that won't be crowing tomorrow morning.

KARL: I don't think you were so clever. You drew blood. He'll never say you did it. I'll be blamed. If word gets to the Quartermaster, I won't get my old job back.

ILSE: You'll be in danger of becoming an honest man.

KARL: What I do is honest even if it's not legal. Let's not squabble. OK. Try to understand, just for a minute. Four months I waited for your visit. You didn't come. But every night and morning I said, I love you.

ILSE: As you looked in the mirror.

KARL: I was saying it to you. You must've heard me.

ILSE: No. I wasn't listening.

KARL: Oh, well. I'll say it now, then. I love you.

ILSE: Did you think that would bowl me over?

KARL: I'd need a tank for that.

ILSE: So you've used your biggest guns and I'm still standing.

KARL: I did hope for a slight crack.

ILSE: I'm broken already. My brother loved freedom and was killed fighting for one tyrant against another. As a child I played with him amongst the birch trees and now their shadows are crowded with the ghosts of the butchered. The fields have been fertilised with blood and bone. All for love. I'll never see my family again because they're slaves. At every gate and doorway there stands a stinking heavy-booted Russian guard. He stands there for love. I run from it for my life.

KARL: Is it all right if I still like you? Tell you what, come to the United States with me. With your looks you could be in movies. Film stars don't have to love anyone. You could be a second Garbo.

ILSE: Would you really take me?

KARL: I'd have to send for you. That'd be best. I'd set myself up in a nice little business.

ILSE: And I'd have to wait here.

KARL: It wouldn't be for long. Anyone can be a businessman in America. In no time flat the dough will be rolling in. I'll wear a smart suit, smoke Havana cigars and drink bourbon out of crystal, no ice.

ILSE: You still sound like a bootlegger.

KARL: Prohibition's over. That went out with Al Capone.

ILSE: I heard he's dead, so there's plenty of room for another crook if you get into the country.

KARL: They've no good reason to refuse me.

ILSE: Except that you've just spent time in their gaols.

[KARL *gets his suitcase.*]

KARL: I'm not a thief or murderer. I'd better go see about this job. Business depends on it. I'll see you tonight.

ILSE: If I'm not here, I'll be in Australia .

KARL: I'll take you dancing.

[*He kisses her.*] Don't go biting any more Americans, they're on our side.

[*He goes.*]

ILSE: They're on your side.

SCENE EIGHT

North Queensland, 1845. A clearing. Day. There is the sound of wailing in the distance.

PHILLIPS *rushes on, puffing. He stops to listen. Silence, then the sound of someone crashing through the bush. A magpie calls. The wailing continues.*

PHILLIPS: Johnny! Johnny! This way, boyo. To your left.

[MURPHY *enters carrying a rifle, very excited.*]

MURPHY: Blast! I dropped Mr Gilbert's food.

PHILLIPS: Fuck the food. Where are the women?

MURPHY: I was right behind 'em, Phillips.

PHILLIPS: Yer reckon I've got 'em hid, yer daft monkey? They're probably up some bleedin' gum tree three miles back by now.

[*There is the sound of rustling in the bushes.*]

MURPHY: [*whispering*] That's them. They're here. Real close.

PHILLIPS: [*circling round*] You stay here and block the way. See if yer can't do somethin' right.

MURPHY: [*levelling his rifle*] Don't worry. I'll stop 'em.

PHILLIPS: Put that down. A dead woman's no good to anyone.

[*He goes.*]

MURPHY: I'll just wound them.

[PHILLIPS *yells, off, and* RUTH *rushes on, clothes and hair awry, brandishing a shoe. She sees* MURPHY *and stops.*]

MURPHY: [*hopping about*] Coo-ee! Coo-ee! We got one. We got one in hand.

PHILLIPS: [*off*] There was two in the bush so hang on.

[ILSE *staggers on.*]

MURPHY: [*Hopping about*] Oh God. Oh god, look at 'em. Black as the devil himself.

[ILSE *turns to go back but* PHILLIPS *cuts off her escape. The women should be near to exhaustion as should the men.*]

PHILLIPS: [*to* MURPHY] Move slowly. We don't want 'em chargin' off again. [*To women*] Easy now, easy. We aren't going to hurt you.

RUTH: The GIs are our friends.

ILSE: They think we're German women, that they can have us for nothing. [*To men*] Nicht Deutsche, nicth Deutsche.

RUTH: Freunden.

MURPHY: Jabberin' away. They're frightened of us.

PHILLIPS: We aren't viney-viney ladies, just white men with white cocks.

MURPHY: How's the two of us goin' to hold them down?

PHILLIPS: Do it right we won't have to. Put that rifle down. There's no pleasure in fuckin' a woman that's got shot. [MURPHY *puts the rifle down*] Now back 'em into the trees. Gently now, gently.

[KARL *enters with suitcase. Stops and watches as the women are herded back.*]

MURPHY: Oh Jesus, those bossoms, can't we start yet?

PHILLIPS: Talk to 'em, calm 'em. Like a skittish horse.

MURPHY: Whoa there boy. I mean, thatta girl.

RUTH: He's only a boy playing with himself.

ILSE: [*Holding out her hand*] Make them pay.

PHILLIPS: We got 'em now. Give 'em your buttons. Go on, rip 'em off.

[MURPHY *frantically rips off his buttons and lunges for* RUTH. *They grab both women roughly to stop them running off.*]

MURPHY: Oh God, oh God, oh noo!

PHILLIPS: Too bad boyo. You can watch me.

ILSE: [*As* KARL *turns to go*] Karl!

RUTH: Karl!

PHILLIPS: Karl karl karl! Like bleedin' crows.

SCENE NINE

North Queensland, 1948. The cane field. Day. There is the sound of cane-cutting. It gradually fades and then comes back and stops just before the men appear.

ILSE *and* RUTH *enter carrying food baskets and a billy of tea.*

LYDIA: [*off*] Wait! Can't you? Wait. I can't keep up.

ILSE: [*stopping*] Wear something sensible on your feet.

LYDIA: [*off*] Like you're wearing? Oops! No thank you. I have never seen anything so ugly in my life. They make your feet look like a couple of flounders. I don't know how Karl can let you walk around like that.

RUTH: You mean Otto forces you to dress like that?

ILSE: Even in Latvia no one walked across a field in what you're wearing on your feet.

RUTH: Unless they were drunk and coming home from a dance.

LYDIA: [*joining them*] I didn't walk across fields. I left that to the peasants. I had a nice little shop in Madona and sold china and the most delicate glasses. Before the peasants came into the shop I made them take their boots off at the door and they had to stand in the middle of the room so that their coats and thick hands wouldn't bump the pieces. They could point to what they wanted to look at and I would hold it up before them.

[RUTH *hands* LYDIA *half a dozen pannikins on a string.*]

RUTH: Then you must be the best person to take care of these.

ILSE: Now that you have to point for things in shops here, you're finding out how the peasants felt.

LYDIA: For iron. Everything is iron. Iron houses, iron cups, iron plates.

[*She drops the cups. They clatter.*]

They don't break. You can't even get rid of them.

RUTH: Don't drop them in the dirt.

LYDIA: We live in the dirt. My Otto had a responsible position as a bookkeeper, and now he is breaking his back like a slave.

ILSE: There was always some clumsy peasant doing the slaving. The food on your table didn't grow in a nice little shop in town.

[*The women put down a cloth and lay out the food.*]

LYDIA: You can't call this ... thing up the road a town. Half of it made of iron like our barracks. There is no respite. In Germany we lived in barracks. I could understand that. They were better than these tin drums. When it rains you can't hear. When the sun's out it's a sauna. At night it rains inside from the condensation.

[*She is on the verge of tears of frustration.*]

RUTH: You'll get used to it. You got used to much worse in the war.

LYDIA: If this is peace, I'd rather be shot. I don't want to get used to it. Maybe it's all right for peasants.

ILSE: I'm no more at home here than you are. I don't like the jungles and stinking mud or blood-sucking insects any more than you do. I don't understand this country and it doesn't understand me. I don't like the way men become raw-boned and vulgar and I am afraid that I'll become tired and resentful like its women. But I can live in an iron shed and eat off an iron plate because it won't always be that way. I'll go back to a city and crystal and china. I don't fight it like you do.

RUTH: [*To* LYDIA, *keeping the peace*] It's not easy, but it's not as bad as you think.

LYDIA: You can say that because your biggest problem is how to get from one bed to another without anyone seeing you. Edvards must be blind.

RUTH: I know what you all think, that I wish Edvards was dead and you hope I will go away before anything unpleasant happens so you won't have to stand by and watch.

ILSE: Hush. You don't know what you're saying.

LYDIA: I'm sorry. It's my fault. I was looking for a way to tell you that I'm moving into town as soon as Otto can find me a little flat. There's electricity. It'll be better than out here.

ILSE: You're leaving us?

LYDIA: You can come with me.

RUTH: There's the men to take care of.

LYDIA: Let them fend for themselves during the week and on the weekend they can come to town.

RUTH: No. I'd never see Leonids except under your noses.

ILSE: A flat would be an extra expense.

LYDIA: Well, you'll come and visit me. We'll have coffee and cake off a linen table cloth with cups and saucers.

ILSE: That'd be nice for a change. But we couldn't come often. We have no transport. You'll be alone a lot unless you mix with the town women.

LYDIA: With them I'm a smiling idiot child who understands nothing.

RUTH: Learn English, Lydia.

LYDIA: I speak English, the way it is taught to us by a Dutchman, but no one understands it. I might as well be talking Dutch.

ILSE: Maybe we are.

LYDIA: [*speaking with an accent*] G'day. Hows ares yous todays?

RUTH: Bloody crooks in za guts.

ILSE: That's not English, that's the bastard language. I will speak English. 'Ziss is the chair.' No? [*Sitting down*] That's all there is to it. 'Ziss is the floors.

LYDIA: Zat is a doors

RUTH: Ze teas is on the tables.' It doesn't help when you have to show the butcher you want some spicy sausages. You should have seen his face.

LYDIA: You should have done that Aboriginal dance for him. Then his eyes would really have popped out.

[*She sings with an accent and actions.*]

You put the right hip in,
You put the right hip out,
You put the right hip in
And you shake it all about.
You do the hokey-pokey
And knees-bend, knees-bend.
That's what it's all about.

[ILSE *and* RUTH *laugh and join in. The dance becomes more risque and abandoned as they do front side and backside, nearly collapsing with laughter. The dance is accompanied by the rhythmic sound of the approaching cane cutters. They enter during the last verse, black with soot and burnt sugar. Their eyes gleam whitely as they watch.*]

EDVARDS: OK. You women are having a good time.

RUTH: And why not?

[*The women take the men damp cloths so they can clean their faces and hands.* LEONIDS *just sits and runs a file over his cane knife.*]

KARL: Where did you learn such a dance?

ILSE: At English classes. You'd be surprised what you'd learn about your body.

KARL: My body teaches me all I need to know by how it feels and what it feels.

ILSE: So long as you're satisfied.

KARL: I'll let you know when I'm not.

[ILSE *goes to* LEONIDS. *She cleans his face.*]

ILSE: You haven't cleaned your face. Let me. You'll feel better.

LEONIDS: You think the others would bother if you didn't do it?

ILSE: That's why we do it. To stop you living hand to mouth.

[*The men eat and drink, sitting on the ground. The women stand.*]

OTTO: You should see this field. Twisted cane and stones as big as a man's head. It's murder. My hands are numb and I've got blisters again.

EDVARDS: Of the three farms we've cut, OK, this has got to be absolutely the worst. Bourke swindled you, Karl.

KARL: You've worked three farms and already you're an expert.

EDVARDS: It takes longer to teach an ox how to pull a plough than it does to teach a man to bend his back and swing a knife.

LYDIA: The price is too low if Otto has to pay with the skin of his hands.

KARL: Leonids and I aren't finding it so hard.

LEONIDS: Whichever way you cut it, it's money in the bank.

EDVARDS: OK. So it's two stallions against one clerk and a man of badly knitted parts. Explain to this dumb soldier, OK, why we aren't cutting the tonnage we usually do.

ILSE: Because you were drunk last night.

RUTH: Karl bought the booze, Ilse.

EDVARDS: [*To* KARL] You're the expert price fixer. Re-negotiate. OK. You're the one who was swindled.

KARL: If that's what you think, then we've all been swindled.

LEONIDS: Maybe that's so. But maybe you're up to your old tricks and taking a bit off the top. You're not one to give beer away.

KARL: Remember that next time you drink it.

ILSE: Why don't you sort it out with Bourke. He's on his way. You better eat up or he'll be taking the food out of your mouth as well.

LYDIA: [*passing around the sandwiches*] Here, Otto. Make sure you have some.

[*The men take one or two sandwiches each. There are some they don't touch*]

EDVARDS: No, thanks. [*Speaking with an accent*] No cornered beef. OK. Pure salt.

OTTO: If that meat comes from a cow, it's a sea cow.

RUTH: We've roasted it, stewed it, fried it and grilled it. What else are we supposed to do with it? Boil it?

LEONIDS: Don't buy it again. It's our money you're wasting.

ILSE: Leave them for Mr Bourke. See what he makes of them.

BOURKE: [*off*] Hello there, missus.

ILSE: Yes. Good day.

[BOURKE *enters. He is carrying two bandicoots by the tail.*]

BOURKE: G'day, boys.

[*The men eat.* KARL *waves.*]

Ladies.

RUTH: Hows ares yous?

BOURKE: Pretty bloody good.

[BOURKE *holds the bandicoots up.* LYDIA *shrieks and hides behind* RUTH.]

What d'ya reckon about these bandicoots?

LYDIA: Rats!

BOURKE: Always set a couple of snares when I burn off.

LYDIA: Rats! Look at the size of those rats. They'd carry off babies.

[BOURKE *advances.* RUTH *and* LYDIA *back off, squealing and laughing.*]

RUTH: No. Take them away. Ugh! What a size. What kind of rat is it?

BOURKE: Bloody good tucker. One is enough for me. [*turning to* ILSE] What about you, missus? Game to try one?

[*He holds one out.* ILSE *backs away, shaking her head.*]

ILSE: What does he want me to do with it?

LEONIDS: What to do with rat?

BOURKE: [*laughing*] Rat. No. Bandicoot. Fresh meat. Good to eat.

LEONIDS: No. No. Please.

BOURKE: Suit yourself.

[*He puts the bandicoots in the cane in the shade.*]

ILSE: [*laughing*] He eats rats? We were lucky to get baked beans on toast the first night. We might have had rat. We wouldn't have got over it.

[*They all laugh.*]

EDVARDS: And we thought we had it hard in the war eating cats and dogs.

LYDIA: The man is raving mad.

BOURKE: What's the big joke, eh?

[*The laughter subsides.*]

ILSE: You eat rats!

BOURKE: Ha bloody ha. Bandicoots, yes.

[*The D.P.s laugh and shake their heads in disbelief.*]

You don't know what you're missing out on. A man can live right off the land here.

RUTH: Yous like tea?

BOURKE: Ta. Wouldn't mind a cup.

[RUTH *pours him a cup.*]

OTTO: Give him a sandwich now.

ILSE: No wait a bit. Eat. Make him feel hungry. When there's food he's just around the corner. If you want a new chimney for the stove or a new door hinge, he's not to be found.

LEONIDS: He overcharges for the barracks and we have to feed him as well.

KARL: What are you going to do with all the money you're saving?

LEONIDS: Buy nothing from you.

BOURKE: [*standing over them*] Speak English. Nattering away like monkeys. Bloody rude. So is eating in front of guests.

OTTO: The man's a miser. He'd squeeze a fart out of a dead man.

BOURKE: Just as bloody well I didn't sign you for the conversation. I reckon they made a mistake keepin' you all together. If they'd split you up amongst some Ities or Yugoslavs, you wouldn't be so chirpy. Still you work cheap. I got a real find in Karl.

ILSE: [*offering him a sandwich*] Mr Bourke. Eat.

BOURKE: [*taking one*] Thought you'd never ask. Ta.

ILSE: Eat. Plenty.

[*He takes another.*]

BOURKE: Thanks, missus. Very decent of you. Greedy buggers.

[*They watch him.*]

Ah! Corned beef!

[*He bites heartily into the sandwich, chews, sucks in a breath, looks to spit it out and realises they are watching.*]

ILSE: Good? Yes?

BOURKE: [*pained*] Yes, good! Very bloody salty!

[*The D.P.s laugh softly. They eat and drink, watching.*]

RUTH: Eat! Eat!

BOURKE: I'm eating! See. Oh God. How did you cook this? With salt?

[*He gulps his tea.*]

ILSE: [*offering him another sandwich*] You take more. Eat plenty.

BOURKE: [*taking another*] Very nice! I'll keep this one for later. Thanks.

[*Thinking he has found a way out*]

Cheep-cheep-cheep-cheep. Pretty little birds, them.

[*He throws half a sandwich.*]

ILSE: No, no! You eat!

[*The D.P.s laugh and encourage him. 'Eat! Eat!'*]

BOURKE: Think you're bloody funny, don't ya?

LYDIA: Your cane. No good.

BOURKE: Eh? What would you know, Princess Muck?

OTTO: [*knitting his fingers*] Tangle up! Stones! Break hands. Look!

[*He shows his hands.*]

BOURKE: Yeah. Nice set of blisters. You hold cane-knife too tight. Too tight.

[*He clenches his hand.*]

Best thing for 'em, pardon the French, is piss.

[*The D.P.s look at each other, eyebrows raised.*]

What'd I say now?

EDVARDS: Piss?

BOURKE: Yeah! Piss. I reckon you got the same bodily functions as us. A number one. You know. *Numero uno?* Ah. Come here, Karl.

[KARL *comes to* BOURKE. *They face away from the group.*]

Here! Hold this sandwich for a minute.

[BOURKE *then goes through a charade of undoing his fly, taking out his penis and cupping his hands underneath. He whistles.*]

KARL: He's washing his hands, Otto. Urinating on them.

[*The D.P.s laugh.*]

LYDIA: I've seen enough.

KARL: [*explaining quietly to* BOURKE] Piss. My country. Mean fucks.

BOURKE: Fair go, eh? [*Shrugging*] Maybe that works as well.

[KARL *tries to return the sandwich.*]

You keep the sandwich. You've had your little joke. Get 'em back to work. [*Pointing*] Looks like rain building up over there.

[*They all look.*]

Rain. You cut cane faster. Presto, presto.

LEONIDS: No.

BOURKE: Eh? What d'ya mean, no?

[*They look to* KARL. KARL *shrugs.*]

EDVARDS: Cane is bent. Plenty stones.

LEONIDS: Price no good.

BOURKE: Bullshit! You're getting a bloody good price. And there's bugger all wrong with the cane.

LEONIDS: Cane Inspector comes.

BOURKE: No need. A couple of wild pigs might've got amongst the cane. Nothing more. I don't give a bugger if you have to work in the rain. Karl, sort these bastards out. Get 'em back to work. What the hell do I pay you for?

LEONIDS: [*to* KARL] You fixed the price. Re-negotiate.

[*Pause.*]

EDVARDS: How do you like that? Our crook won't deal with theirs.

KARL: I don't know what you expect. I don't speak the language any better than you. In Germany I could speak German and I traded on the black market which was German. It's time you all started looking after yourselves. I won't always be around to strike the bargains.

[*The group start talking all at once.*]

LEONIDS: What bargains have you made for yourself?

ILSE: Ask him about the chimney for the stove.

OTTO: Price no good.

EDVARDS: The door hinge is broken. Door no good.

RUTH: [*to* LEONIDS] Ask him for a new mattress.

LYDIA: Otto. I want to go to stay in town as soon as possible.

LEONIDS: Money for barracks. Too much.

BOURKE: [*waving his arms*] All right! All right! Jesus Christ! You found them words quick enough. Karl is ganger, right?

[*The D.P.s nod.*]

Together [*putting his arm around* KARL] we make price. Fair price.

KARL: You pay sixpence more a ton, OK?

BOURKE: Not on your bleeding life. [*Aside to* KARL] If you're with them, Karl, you can forget our little deal.

KARL: [*to the others*] He says it's a fair price and I'm inclined to think it's not so bad. At the end of the season we'll want to go out on a good note. If we go along with him, we should be able to rent the barracks fairly cheaply in the slack.

LYDIA: I'm not staying one week more.

LEONIDS: Call cane inspector. We talk.

BOURKE: Too much bloody talk. Bloody Bolsheviks.

[LEONIDS *starts to go for* BOURKE. *'Bolshevik' is the supreme insult.*]

EDVARDS: No Bolsheviks! We no work! Call cane inspector!

BOURKE: Your leadership is worth a pinch of piss, Karl. You've just done your bonus. From now on you get the same as them. You call me a cheat when I give you a good deal. The whole country opens their hearts to you and you rub salt into them. Well, make the most of what you've got. Next year you not so damn lucky. This good job, this good money. Go to Englishmen. Much as I hate 'em, at least they speak the same language. Understand? Next year. You no cut cane. No easy money. English migrant cut cane. You go to buggery.

KARL: We have contract.

BOURKE: You break. You give me word you cut. Now you no work.

KARL: We have two years contract.

BOURKE: Your contract's with the Government. Not with me. They can find you something else. Railways. Choo-choo. Timber cutting. Chopchop. You're getting it easy this year. Bloody good job. Thrown away. No wonder you lost the war.

[*He starts to go.*]

KARL: We talk to cane inspector.

BOURKE: Get fucked.

EDVARDS: Hey! You forget. Rats!

[EDVARDS *tosses them off after him. There is some bitter laughter and a brief silence.*]

ILSE: What did he say to you about a bonus?

KARL: What business is that of yours?

ILSE: It's everybody's business.

KARL: As we're not working we won't get one, simple.

LEONIDS: You said nothing about a bonus for us.

OTTO: It was never mentioned in the price.

EDVARDS: Because our little businessman was the only one to get one. OK? For the good deal he did for Mr Bourke.

KARL: [*shrugging*] You always got a fair price from me. See if you can do better. I get no thanks for my pains.

LEONIDS: Except what you could rake off the top.

EDVARDS: OK. We wait. The cane inspector will come and we'll get a better price. Bourke needs us to cut his cane.

KARL: This year, anyway. And next year?

LEONIDS: The sawmills are always looking for men to cut timber.

OTTO: Oh no. From cutting sticks to chopping trees.

KARL: This is what you wanted. Our name will be shit for cane-cutting. But there's plenty of timber-cutting.

RUTH: What happens to us?

EDVARDS: You'll stay in town. You'll like that. OK. We have to stay in a camp and come to town on weekends.

RUTH: While we sit and wait.

KARL: You're all good at waiting.

OTTO: If you hadn't tried to swindle us–

[KARL *goes.*]

ILSE: Where are you going now?

KARL: I'll do my waiting at the hotel. When they fix a price, they can come and find me.

[*He goes.*]

EDVARDS: I wait better with a drink. Come on, Leonids.

[OTTO *starts off with them.*]

LYDIA: Otto.

OTTO: If I have a beer or two I'll make medicine for my hands.

[*The men go, laughing. The women sing:*]

Don't ask me, now, what makes love fade and die', friend

That's something I have tried to comprehend .
Why was it that the summer spell was broken?
Ask no more, friend, there's no more that I know.
Why was it that the summer spell was broken?
Ask no more, friend, there's no more that I know.

[*The women go during the last few lines of the song.*]

END OF PART ONE

PART TWO

SCENE ONE

North Queensland, 1948. Night. KARL *stands smoking a cigarette.*

LYDIA *enters.*

LYDIA: [*calling softly*] Otto! Are you there? Karl!
KARL: Yes?
LYDIA: Have you seen Otto?
KARL: No.
LYDIA: I woke up and he wasn't there.
KARL: Don't worry yourself, he can't have gone far., I'm sure he will be back shortly. Stay here with me.
LYDIA: What are you doing? Stop it. Karl!

[*She backs away from him.*]

KARL: You can't be happy with that weed.
LYDIA: Otto!

[ILSE *enters.*]

ILSE: What's going on?
KARL: Lydia has lost Otto.
ILSE: How lost him?
LYDIA: He's gone; not in bed.
KARL: The blacks took him.
ILSE: Don't be stupid. We'll go and find him.

[ILSE *leads* LYDIA. KARL *shrugs and follows.*]

LEICHHARDT: [*off*] Go on! Idiot! Go round further.

[OTTO *stumbles on. The sound of horses is heard.*]

Cut them off. Cretin. You never saw horses before? Take a hold. By the mane or by the tail.

[OTTO *advances, hand outstretched.*]

OTTO: [*nervously*] There, boy. There you go. Come here. Time to go to work. The fields have to be mowed. Can't stand idle all day growing a big belly.

[*He stops.*]

Hey up! Don't go.

LEICHHARDT: [*off*] Why are you standing? Idiot. You can wait all day and it won't come to you. Run at them. Run now! Arrgh!

[*There is the sound of horses wheeling and leaping away. An old saddle comes flying through the air.* LEICHHARDT *enters bent double.*]

You thick shithead! You caused me to be kicked in the stomach. When you run, run. The animals are smarter than you.

OTTO: I don't know horses.

LEICHHARDT: That is painfully obvious to me. This time you will take him round the neck and hold him till I put this saddle on. If you flinch I'll see you walk across Australia with bloody footsteps. Stand still and I will drive the horse to you.

[*He starts to run, swinging the saddle.*]

Arrgh! Yah! Dumbest creatures on God's earth. Come on. Arrgh!

[*He throws the saddle off. The other D.P.s enter.* EDVARDS *and* OTTO *stand fast watching the horse shy away.*]

EDVARDS: Horses.

LEONIDS: How come we no longer know the sound of horses?

ILSE: They are beautiful in the moonlight. Just like home.

LYDIA: Otto! Otto! Why doesn't he come!

RUTH: He is sleepwalking. We mustn't wake him suddenly.

EDVARDS: [*laughing*] I can bring him back. [*Calling like a drill sergeant*] Private Otto Bernhards. Attention.

[OTTO *snaps to attention.*]

LEONIDS: Did you see that?

LYDIA: He's acting the clown again. Otto!

EDVARDS: Perhaps not. You wouldn't think that men at the front would sleepwalk but they did, OK. Up herding cows, gathering firewood, mowing fields. If they were lucky you could talk them back to the trenches. [*Calling* OTTO] About turn! Quick march! Hup two! Hup two! Hup two! Right turn' Hup two! Hup two! OK.

KARL: I didn't know he could drill so well. Left turn! Hup two! Hup two!

[*The men laugh. They all give commands.* OTTO *grows frantic trying to follow them*]

LYDIA: Otto! Stop it! Come back. [*To the men*] Stop it! Please stop!

EDVARDS: Halt! Surrender! You are surrounded.

[OTTO *puts his hands up.*]

RUTH: Bring him back, Edvards. Leonids, for God's sake make them stop.

EDVARDS: Just having a bit of fun.

[LYDIA *goes to meet him.*]

LYDIA: Otto wake up! The game's over.

[*Slapping his face gently*] Wake up!

OTTO: What! Are you– Where are the horses?

LYDIA: Where are the horses, indeed. Over there.

LEONIDS: [*laughing*] He was only fooling.

OTTO: I have to catch the horses for the German.

[*The men laugh.*]

ILSE: Take him to bed. It was only a dream.

[RUTH *and* LYDIA *lead* OTTO *away.*]

KARL: Nice act, Otto.

ILSE: [*to the men*] You should be ashamed of yourselves.

KARL: [*laughing*] Why? What did we do? He was only fooling.

LEONIDS: Tomorrow he'll probably be laughing at us.

ILSE: Of course that makes it all right. One of us has some trouble, the rest of us stand back and laugh. Because tomorrow the roles will be reversed. Who else can we turn to but each other? And when we do there will be a line of mocking faces. Mindlessly clucking hens.

EDVARDS: [*mocking* ILSE] OK. So let nobody call wolf. Hup two! Hup two!

SCENE TWO

Both camps: North Queensland, 1845, and Stuttgart, 1947. Night.

PHILLIPS: [*off*] Hello, the camp.

[PHILLIPS *and* MURPHY *enter*]

LEICHHARDT: So the hunters return. With empty hands.

PHILLIPS: [*sniffing*] What's cooking?

GILBERT: Dead dog.

MURPHY: Phew! What a pong.

PHILLIPS: It's putrid. Are you sure it wasn't ill, Doctor?

LEICHHARDT: You are not obliged to eat it and there is not enough for four men.

GILBERT: There's nothing else.

LEICHHARDT: Eat your specimens. Always teensy little birds. Half a mouthful. Why don't you find something the size or an elephant?

GILBERT: Elephant? So we're in Africa now? The way you use a sextant we'll be in London in a month. There has to be an easier way to Port Essington than strolling to the tip of Australia and turning left.

LEICHHARDT: You are not hungry, that is obvious. A hungry man always finds food.

PHILLIPS: Not if there's none to be found, sir.

GILBERT: It's about time you faced the facts; we're out of supplies, game is scarce and you don't know where we are.

LEICHHARDT: You hope to turn me back, but I am not so easily fooled. To a man you dream of sea coasts and ships and lust for the easy pleasures. But no man starves in paradise, so what are you afraid of?

GILBERT: Of stupidity and the senseless waste of life and work. What we've learned has no value unless we share it.

LEICHHARDT: If it's your bird skins you are worried about, strap them to your back and fly to safety. We will make better progress without your burden.

GILBERT: Phillips and John Murphy have the right to determine their own fate.

LEICHHARDT: A convict and a mere boy who joined me because they could not make good otherwise. What you are you owe to me. Phillips, you must go on to win a pardon.

PHILLIPS: A pardon won't profit me if I'm lyin' dead in a swamp, Doctor. I'm with Mr Gilbert.

LEICHHARDT: Shame them, Johnny. Show them how a boy can make cowards of men. Come beside me.

MURPHY: I'm not a boy any more an' I'm for followin' the marked trees back the way we came.

LEICHHARDT: The trees are not an avenue for retreat.

GILBERT: Three to one against. We go back, all of us.

LEICHHARDT: Thick-headed louts. What pissy little lives in so vast a place. In the morning we go on. To discipline you I will not share my catch.

[LEICHHARDT *takes the dog and stalks off*]

PHILLIPS: If yer want to discipline us, you'd make us eat that stinkin' dog.

MURPHY: We can't go back without him. They'll say we did him in.

GILBERT: We'll see in the morning. If you're hungry, there's some bird carcasses to make up a thin soup.

[*A shaft of light spills across the stage as from a doorway. An accordian plays a waltz.* KARL *and* RUTH *dance into the light.* RUTH *stumbles on the rough ground and stops.* KARL *holds her.* GILBERT *watches* RUTH.]

RUTH: I'm giddy. You certainly lost none of your flair for the dance while you were in goal. Who did you practise with? A G.I.?

KARL: With my pillow. No substitute for the arm of a warm woman. How about a kiss?

RUTH: [*a peck*] There.

KARL: Is that all?

RUTH: I came out here for the air. Imagine if you had to pay for every breath.

KARL: I haven't been able to acquire the franchise. When I do, I'll make a killing.

RUTH: Several at your prices.

KARL: You'll always be good for a discount.

RUTH: Ka-arl! Don't, you're drunk.

KARL: So what? Did I step on your feet? No. I dance better when I'm drunk. I do most things better when I'm drunk.

RUTH: Stop it. Ilse's my friend.

KARL: I'm your friend too. Don't worry about Ilse. She blows hot and cold.

RUTH: Look, I'm not going to warm you up. I'm married.

KARL: Almost twice over.

RUTH: You're a pig of a man.

[RUTH *turns to go back inside.* ILSE *comes out into the light.*]

ILSE: [*to* RUTH] Leonids is waiting over by the trees.

[RUTH *goes to* LEONIDS. *They embrace.*]

KARL: Hey, where's she going?

ILSE: It's none of your business, businessman.

KARL: That's Leonids. Edvards is in there.

ILSE: Getting drunker and winning the war. He has several campaigns to fight before he looks for his bed.

KARL: Come inside and dance.

ILSE: I'm watching for Ruth.

KARL: She'll be a while.

[LEONIDS *and* RUTH *start to go.*]

MURPHY: [*stopping them*] Mr Gilbert?

[KARL *and* ILSE *dance close in the light* RUTH *waits.*]

Mr Gilbert, I can't take your soup. I ate this afternoon at a natives' camp. I was bringing some back for you, but I dropped it.

GILBERT: Never mind. [*Sniffing*] You smell different.

MURPHY: I had a wash.

GILBERT: That must be it.

MURPHY: In the lagoon. Took all me clothes off and had a right old scrub, all over.

GILBERT: And lost all your buttons in the process. You'll find some spares in my kit.

[LEONIDS *goes to join* RUTH]

MURPHY: Mr Gilbert ... I'll turn down your bedroll.

GILBERT: Thanks, Johnny.

[KARL *and* ILSE *stop dancing.* LEONIDS *lies down on* GILBERT'*s bed,* RUTH *sits astride him. They make love.*]

KARL: What a beautiful dress. I love the way the skirt swings below when you dance. But it's no good dancing out here. It'll ruin your shoes.

[ILSE *laughs. She kisses him quickly. He caresses her breasts.*]

Lovely to touch. Peaches.

[ILSE *gently squeezes* KARL'*s balls.*]

ILSE: Apples.

KARL: [*groaning*] You know what they're up to. Who knows how long they'll be there.

ILSE: You want to time them?

KARL: Not exactly with a clock.

ILSE: No. Not with a clock. [*Making* KARL *squirm.*] You could have been a cavalry officer. Your balls would sit well forward in the saddle.

[KARL *removes his jacket and puts it on the ground for* ILSE. *He kneels.*]

If this ground will ruin my shoes, what will it do to my back? You lie down.

KARL: My back, your knees. You'd ruin your stockings.

[*He runs his hand up her leg.*]

Did I give them to you?

[ILSE *turns her back to him and bends over slightly.*]

ILSE: This way, standing. I can watch the door for Ruth.

[KARL *undoes his flies and lifts her skirts.*]

KARL: Hey, where'd you get this suspender belt?

ILSE: Look, are you taking an inventory or what?

KARL: No, no. But it's good stuff. High quality, like you. A man can't help noticing. High quality.

ILSE: Get on with it. Four months without and you want to chatter. Have you forgotten how to–

[*Grunting.*]

Wait.

KARL: Yes, no. Stop, go. Oh God!

[*By now,* RUTH *rests beside* LEONIDS.]

MURPHY: Mr Gilbert.

GILBERT: What is it now?

MURPHY: I'll repay you, Mr Gilbert. I owe you so much and to think when I dropped that food, I didn't even look for it.

GILBERT: When there's no food, it's best not to dwell on it. The same goes for beer, tobacco and women.

ILSE: [*to* KARL] It's nothing. Go slowly.

MURPHY: I was lookin' out for meself, for me own pleasures ... with some native women ... I gave 'em the buttons ... for ... you know ...

GILBERT: Cultural exchange.

MURPHY: It was me first time.

GILBERT: You're certain to remember it.

MURPHY: I didn't mean to hurt them.

KARL: [*groaning*] I can't ...

ILSE: It's all right.

GILBERT: When you're in the desert you want water. At sea you pine for the shore. Completeness. God gave Adam a woman for that reason. Go to bed. Man. We have an early start.

MURPHY: G'night, Mr Gilbert.

[LEONIDS *goes with* RUTH. *She leans back against a tree and they fuck standing up.* LEONIDS *has his back to us.* MURPHY *and* PIIILLIPS *bed down.*]

ILSE: Give me your handkerchief. What a flood.

KARL: Classy underwear.

ILSE: You still going on about that.

KARL: I didn't give them to you.

ILSE: I traded for them. You're not the only black marketeer in Stuttgart.

KARL: Too true. On the way over to get my job, I saw some G.I.s with two of our women.

ILSE: Lots of 'our women' go with soldiers.

KARL: I suppose so. I never really noticed before.

ILSE: They learn some English, get a bottle of perfume and if they're unlucky, they get a baby as well.

KARL: You think it's a joke?

ILSE: Yes. A joke on all women.

KARL: It looked rough to me.

ILSE: The war isn't over for some of us.

KARL: I want to marry you, Ilse.

ILSE: No.

KARL: No? Why not?

ILSE: Men and women live separately in this camp and have to steal pleasures like thieves.

KARL: What's the difference? Man and wife or lovers?

ILSE: We're more like dogs in heat grappling in the dark under trees.

KARL: I really mean it.

ILSE: There's no point discussing it. I'm going to Australia and you're off to Chicago to drink bourbon from Garbo's shoe.

KARL: I've changed my mind.

ILSE: Why? Didn't you get your job back?

KARL: I didn't go. When I saw those two women with the G.I.s I had to turn away. I was afraid, for a moment, that one of the women was you, you and Ruth.

ILSE: What if it had been me? When that G.I. prodded me today like a cow in a paddock, you stood by hoping to profit from the exchange. When nothing comes of it, you ask me to marry you as if you owned the cow all along. 'Our women'. You work like a pimp.

KARL: Have you ever gone with them?

ILSE: You want to know how I came by this underwear? The same way I got this dress, the way you get cigarettes and razor blades and whisky ...

KARL: I trade for them.

ILSE: With gold teeth. But a woman has to keep her teeth to keep her looks. If she keeps her looks, she can sell that soft part of her, even though men are sure it has teeth.

KARL: When I was in gaol?

ILSE: And before.

KARL: You needed food, clothes.

ILSE: I wanted for nothing.

KARL: They raped you, then.

ILSE: No. I went willingly.

KARL: I don't believe you.

ILSE: This afternoon you wanted to believe it was me and Ruth. You can believe it of me. Leave Ruth out of it.

KARL: What damn difference does that make when she's out there with Leonids?

ILSE: That's right. Shout. Tell everyone.

KARL: Everyone knows except Edvards.

[*Pause.*]

They all know about you too. All except me.

[*He slaps her.*]

Tell me they raped you.

ILSE: I raped them. I tried, anyway. I gave up. It was a losing battle. I wanted to break them on my body and all I did was confuse them.

KARL: [*slapping her*] Tell me!

ILSE: As mother, whore, mistress or wife? It's not easy to be a woman when boys become men by taking a life or two. They never know exactly what they want.

KARL: I'll kill you, you slut.

[RUTH *and* LEONIDS *come back into the light.*]

RUTH: Ilse, Karl. What's going on? Calm down.

KARL: You stay away from me. As if you don't know. 'Lover boy'. What a laugh, eh?

LEONIDS: [*from the shadows*] Go inside and have a drink before you wake the whole camp.

KARL: [*to* LEONIDS] You sure wouldn't like that, would you? Don't want to wake the dead, eh Ruthie? I'll fix them. I'll string their arseholes on a fence like dried apples. The bloody unknown soldiers.

[KARL *goes.*]

RUTH: What on earth did you say to him?

ILSE: Not much.

[*The shaft of light snaps out. The dance music is replaced by the soft wailing of native women.* LEICHHARDT *comes from the trees.*]

GILBERT: There's been some interference with the native women. I think we should have a guard on the camp tonight.

LEICHHARDT: Is it customary for a private soldier to make suggestions to his general?

GILBERT: I'm not in any bloody army.

LEICHHARDT: Bully for you or you'd be shot for desertion. I am still the leader.

GILBERT: Any man who can eat a rotten dog and then spend the best part of an hour vomiting in the undergrowth is no longer fit to lead.

LEICHHARDT: It is my destiny and you will not cheat it from me.

GILBERT: As you have clearly gone mad, we are restoring some sanity to proceedings–

LEICHHARDT: By molesting the native women. What a fine beginning you have made.

GILBERT: I said nothing about molesting.

LEICHHARDT: If I am mad, how is it that you see the nightmares? I wish you sweeter dreams, Mr Gilbert.

[LEICHHARDT *beds down.* GILBERT *does so on the other side of the fire. As the men settle, dark figures carrying pieces of timber approach stealthily from the trees. The attack begins. It is as though a spear had been thrown into camp.* MURPHY *screams and tries to roll away. The attackers disperse.*]

Native attack! Gun caps! Quick. Gun caps. Attack. We're being attacked.

[*They all grab for their rifles. There is confusion and mayhem.*]

MURPHY: Me rifle's not loaded.

GILBERT: Load it, for Christ's sake.

[GILBERT *gets between* MURPHY *and the attackers and tries to bring his rifle to bear.* LEICHHARDT *fires at the attackers.*]

LEICHHARDT: Fire! I hit one.

[GILBERT *drops to his knees clutching at his chest.* LEICHHARDT *and* PHILLIPS *fire after the attackers.*]

KARL: Provos! Run - Get out of here.

OTTO: The others–

KARL: Forget them! Move!

GILBERT: Here, Johnny. Take my gun. The bastard killed me.

[*He laughs.* MURPHY *takes the rifle follows attackers. Then all is quiet.* GILBERT *lies by the fire. He coughs.*]

G.I. SAM: Come back and fight! Chicken livered bastards.

[MURPHY *returns to* GILBERT'*s side.*]

LEICHHARDT: [*snapping*] Keep from the light, donkey. You want to die?

MURPHY: Mr Gilbert's dead.

[LEICHHARDT *bends over him.*]

LEICHHARDT: He can't be dead! I must bleed him. Give me a knife.

[PHILLIPS *gives* LEICHHARDT *a knife.* MURPHY *cradles* GILBERT. LEICHHARDT *slashes* GILBERT'*s wrists. He tips* GILBERT'*s head back and slashes a temporal artery.*]

No blood. Too late. His heart is stopped.

MURPHY: Poor Mr Gilbert.

PHILLIPS: What happened? Was he shot?

MURPHY: Me rifle wasn't loaded.

LEICHHARDT: A spear. It must've dislodged as he fell. I didn't see.

MURPHY: Me rifle wasn't loaded.

LEICHHARDT: There is nothing more we can do. We pack up and strike camp now. Work quickly or you will be massacred too.

PHILLIPS: Where're we goin'?

LEICHHARDT: Port Essington.

PHILLIPS: Oh no we ain't. Just tonight we decided to go back. We still outvote you two to one.

LEICHHARDT: Just tonight Mr Gilbert was killed by natives. Something made those natives upset. I say we go now.

MURPHY: Don't argue, Phillips.

[MURPHY *starts to drag* GILBERT *off.*]

LEICHHARDT: What are you doing? It's too late for him.

MURPHY: I'm not leavin' him. I'll bury him in the mornin'.

[*He goes.*]

LEICHHARDT: [*to* PHILLIPS] Take only what is necessary. And Mr Gilbert's specimens.

anthropologist stories. Scientific element

SCENE THREE

Stuttgart, 1947. Night

KARL *waits. He watches* OTTO *tip-toeing in the dark.* KARL *grabs him and throws him down.*

KARL: Come here, clown.

OTTO: It's you!

KARL: Don't wet yourself again. What'll you say to Lydia about your trousers?

OTTO: I'll say I was walking home drunk and I fell in a puddle.

KARL: It hasn't rained here in Stuttgart for weeks. I hate to think what kind of a husband you'll make. You can't even lie convincingly. What'll you do if we wind up in court on a murder charge? Spill your guts?

OTTO: You should've stopped Edvards kicking that Yank when he was down.

KARL: Where are the others?

OTTO: We decided to make our way here separately so we'd be less conspicious.

KARL: If they're tippy-toeing round the place like you were, we'll be behind bars in no time.

[LEONIDS *enters. He says nothing.*]

OTTO: We're just waiting for Edvards.

KARL: [*to* OTTO] Go and see if you can't find him. He's probably out starting World War Three.

OTTO: You started it. Yes, all right, what the hell.

[*He goes.*]

KARL: What are you going to do about Ruth?

LEONIDS: What business is that of yours?

KARL: Edvards is a friend. I don't like it when someone gives his wife a good fucking under a hedge when he's not been back a day.

LEONIDS: Some friend you are to tell him the Americans had been taking advantage of his wife when it wasn't true.

KARL: Can you be sure of that?

[*Pause.*]

I've done you a favour, see. Putting it bluntly, you can get out from underneath .

LEONIDS: I was going to marry Ruth. Who knows? If Edvards killed that Yank, maybe he'll disappear again.

KARL: Don't even think it. If he goes down, we all go with him.

[EDVARDS *and* OTTO *enter.*]

OTTO: Here we are. I don't think anyone saw us.

EDVARDS: All quiet on the western front. OK.

LEONIDS: The war is over, Edvards.

EDVARDS: After one little skirmish. Then let's go home. OK.

OTTO: Did you kill that G.I.?

EDVARDS: The Latvian divisions take no prisoners, Otto.

KARL: Oh good! We go to teach some clever Yanks to keep their hands off our women and because you get carried away, we could end up on a murder charge.

EDVARDS: The way I see it, OK, if you're going to give someone a hiding, you do it properly.

KARL: I can't afford another stretch in gaol on any count.

OTTO: What if they shoot us?

EDVARDS: You die. OK. It's permanent.

KARL: All we have to do is keep our mouths shut and go on like before. We know nothing. We went to the dance, got blind drunk and returned to barracks. That's easy enough to remember.

LEONIDS: [*pointedly at* KARL] And then one night some drunk will start shouting–

KARL: Who cares? We'll be in Australia by then.

OTTO: Are you coming too?

KARL: I'll put my application in tomorrow.

LEONIDS: What about Ruth and Edvards? They're not taking married couples.

KARL: I'll get Edvards some false papers to say he's single.

LEONIDS: Ruth will be a widow again.

KARL: Not for long. She and Edvards can remarry in Australia.

OTTO: A fresh start with a new wife. Like me and Lydia.

EDVARDS: I think Ruth would like another wedding. So that's the future. OK.

KARL: All we have to do is see what can be done about finding a wife for Leonids.

SCENE FOUR

North Queensland, 1949. A clearing surrounded by a river in flood.

LEICHHARDT *stands facing the sunrise.* GILBERT *enters during* LEICHHARDT'*s speech and crouches behind him.* LEICHHARDT *is unaware of* GILBERT'*s presence until* GILBERT *speaks.*

LEICHHARDT: The loveliness of morning just before and after sunrise. The air so clear and transparent. The promised land lies always to the east. Walk to the west and you walk into the hottest fire. With the sun on my back, I walked away from each morning. I saw where each day ended. At night I fell on a soil as unyielding as stone. When I lifted my head my skin was scorched to the ground. My eyes saw nothing. The red of day and black of night. Blinded. The horses fell down and died. Their tongues bloated so large they choked. My body dried out and my mouth filled with sand. Before a man dies, his breath whistles round his ribs as if he were already a skeleton hung in an exotic garden. A wind chime. I have heard my own bones sing.

GILBERT: You deserted me in such a wilderness. You shot me and left me lying in a burnt clearing.

LEICHHARDT: I lit a fire over your grave so the natives would not see the earth had been disturbed.

GILBERT: I was scoured out by a flood. Some natives found me after the flood receded. Not having had so tame a spirit in their clutches before, they opened me up, as I would have liked, to learn my innermost secrets. How disappointed they were to learn the viney-viney was like them. They washed and wrapped my organs in aromatic leaves, filled my body and laid me to rest on a platform in the branches of a tree. Light and airy and warm. A kind of heaven. But the birds gave me no peace and my bones were carried off by wild pigs. I live in dread of rain and floods. At night to get warm, I sit in warm ashes until the sun rises.

LEICHHARDT: Fire and flood! That is the singular character of this remarkable country, extremes so often meet. The coast is luxuriant green. The interior is burnt red.

GILBERT: I've heard all this before. No doubt it was part of your victory speech in Sydney. But did you tell them how you shot me and left me to rot?

LEICHHARDT: That is why I've come, to lead you back to Sydney. But first I must drink. Is there a river nearby?

[*There are sounds of people wading through water.*]

GILBERT: A great flood, an inland sea.

LEICHHARDT: It was promised to me. Wait here. I have logged your position.

GILBERT: With your usual precision. Is there a tree on your horizon?

LEICHHARDT: [*gazing off*] Now that you mention it, yes there is.

GILBERT: [*going*] It's one of yours.

ANGIE: [*off*] Are you sure we're going the right way?

McQUAIDE: [*off*] It's the only way to go. Uphill. Downhill is under water.

ANGIE: [*off*] We've been walking in water for half a mile. Uphill is under water as well.

[*There is a louder splash.*]

Shit! I walked into another hole.

[McQUAIDE *laughs.*]

Let me ride in the boat.

[LEICHHARDT/EDVARDS *looks off, towards the approaching walkers.*]

McQUAIDE: [*off*] It drags on the bottom. Won't be long now. It's getting shallower.

EDVARDS: [*calling*] Hey., Doctor! Where yous go?

McQUAIDE: [*off*] Eddie! We're getting closer than we thought. Go through the trees.

EDVARDS: [*laughing*] You go fishing?

[McQUAIDE *and* ANGIE *enter.* McQUAIDE'*s trousers are rolled up.* ANGIE'*s skirts are tucked up and wet.*]

McQUAIDE: Yeah, we go fishing for men in a timber camp.

EDVARDS: We go to town?

McQUAIDE: No need, mate. Town is very boring. Angie and me thought you must be dry out here so we, brought you something to wet your whistle. You can't be cutting much timber in this weather.

[McQUAIDE *carries a carton of rum and beer*]

EDVARDS: Hello Mrs. McQuaide.

ANGIE: Hello Eddie. Your lot are the best drinking company he ever had. No one else drinks heavily enough.

EDVARDS: Water comes up. OK.

McQUAIDE: Yeah, terrible drink. Can't keep it down, myself.

[OTTO, KARL *and* LEONIDS *enter carrying sandbags. They dump them. The men look very dishevelled.*]

KARL: Good day, Doctor. And Angie.

[KARL *shakes her hand then kisses her.*]

ANGIE: Quaint foreign custom.

[OTTO *and* LEONIDS *smile and nod.*]

McQUAIDE: [*laughing*] He's the only one practising.

KARL: [*to* ANGIE] You are wet.

ANGIE: Very. [*Looking down at her legs*] *Oh, Doc! I've got leeches on me. Doc!*

McQUAIDE: Karl will take care of them.

[ANGIE *lifts her skirts.* KARL *squats and picks the leeches off her legs.* McQUAIDE *opens a fresh bottle and passes it around.* McQUAIDE *sits and drinks heavily.*]

EDVARDS: Look at him. A woman lifts her skirts and he dredges up the old charm from some stinking pit. No pride.

OTTO: Leave him alone. He doesn't get much chance to practise these days.

ANGIE: Ooh! You're very good at that. So gentle.

LEONIDS: Water comes up. Big flood.

McQUAIDE: No need to worry. It won't come any higher.

[KARL *squeezes water from* ANGIE'S *skirt.*]

KARL: Come. We make you dry.

[ANGIE *gets a bottle from* McQUAIDE.]

ANGIE: Karl's going to dry me out.

McQUAIDE: Be right with you.

ANGIE: Don't hurry on my account.

LEONIDS: [*to* KARL] Will you bring more sandbags?

KARL: What's the point digging out the hill on the other side to bring it over here? We're not gaining anything.

LEONIDS: What if we're washed out?

KARL: I'll climb a tree.

LEONIDS: I say we need sandbags. I'm still in charge of this camp.

KARL: That means you get to stay here while we go off in the boat. Get sandbags for yourself.

[KARL *and* ANGIE *go.*]

EDVARDS: He's right. We have a boat now. OK.

OTTO: How come he has all the luck.

EDVARDS: Think of it this way, the worst you'll end up with is a hangover. He could get the pox. Pass me that bottle. OK.

LEONIDS: Are you two going to bring more sandbags?

EDVARDS: I'm going on sick parade. My joints are playing me up.

[EDVARDS *uses some of the rum as rubbing alcohol on his shoulder.*]

OTTO: If the water rises, I'd rather leave. They're not paying us to sit here.

[LEONIDS *goes.*]

McQUAIDE: I've never seen much in the way of war wounds. Nothing as impressive as that. Shrapnel?

EDVARDS: [*speaking with his accent*] English bomb. [*Pointing to his face, chest and stomach*] Here. Here. Here. [*Without an accent*] It smashed this shoulder and the skin was hanging off my face and arm. I pull the skin back. I can see with one eye, but the view is from above. [*With accent*] I float. Outside. See myself. OK. Medic comes. [*No accent*] He finds some small holes. Puts a dressing. And he gets up off his knees, his trousers are soaked in blood. OK. [*With accent*] My blood. On knees. [*No accent*] He sees my back. Big hole. He stuffs his shirt into the hole. And then I feel my body filling up with blood. It filled my throat. [*With accent*] I drown. In blood. OK. [*No accent*] I see myself. Peace. Sleeping on stretcher. A team of doctors stole me away, with masks and bloody hands. [*With accent*] They give me life. Full sentence.

[*During the last part of the speech, there is the distant sound of a chugging motor.* LEONIDS *enters with more sandbags.*]

LEONIDS: Listen. Boat.

[*The motor dies*]

McQUAIDE: Someone making deliveries to the farms. The sound carries a long way over water. From farms. Down below.

OTTO: [*to* McQUAIDE] You are doctor. No?

McQUAIDE: Yes.

OTTO: We find bones. Old bones. From man, or womans.

McQUAIDE: You don't say?

OTTO: And tree. Datum on tree.

McQUAIDE: A blind man could find a tree here.

[OTTO *scratches in the dirt.*]

L one-eight-four-five. You don't say, eh? Could be quite a find, that.

OTTO: I show.

McQUAIDE: Later, later. Let's have a drink first.

[OTTO *goes.*]

LEONIDS: The water is still rising.

EDVARDS: We are only men, OK. We can't turn back the tide. Let's go back to camp where there are chairs to sit on. The least we can do is have a drink, OK, while we watch our ship go down.

[LEONIDS *shakes his head.*]

Suit yourself.

McQUAIDE: Hang on a minute, Eddie. Don't leave me with this bloke. He doesn't drink.

[*They go.* LEONIDS *looks off. We hear the sound of people approaching through the water.*]

BOURKE: [*off*] You coulda stayed in the boat, missus. No need to go exertin' yourself now. Don't want you droppin' the kid on me.

ILSE: [*off*] Is all right. Thanks. I can walk.

BOURKE: [*off*] Ahoy the camp.

[ILSE *and* RUTH *enter, skirts pulled up.* ILSE *is very pregnant.*]

RUTH: [*to* LEONIDS] Look at you. What have you been doing? Two weeks away from civilisation and you're a wild man.

[OTTO *enters to see* RUTH *and* LEONIDS *embrace.* BOURKE *enters.*]

OTTO: Well, look who's here in time for the party. [*With accent*] Good day, Bourkie.

BOURKE: G'day, Otto. Brought some supplies for you fellers. Your women talked me into it when I saw them in town.

[OTTO *takes the bag of food.*]

OTTO: [*to* ILSE] Better call Karl to check for leeches. [*Calling*] Karl! Lydia didn't come up?

ILSE: No. She thought it was too dangerous.

OTTO: Oh, that's a new one. Usually everything is too dirty, too small, or too rough. Now it's too dangerous for her.

[*He goes.*]

BOURKE: If the water keeps rising we all go back to town.

[KARL *and* ANGIE *come from the trees, laughing, unaware of the arrivals.* ANGIE *now wears one of* KARL*'s shirts. It is long enough and baggy enough to be a dress on her. When they see the others, they walk apart guiltily. A brief silence.*]

BOURKE: Hello, Mrs McQuaide. Get caught with your pants down?

ANGIE: [*evenly*] How's the farm, Ollie?

BOURKE: Pretty damn wet. Like your backside.

KARL: Hello, Ilse. You shouldn't be here in your condition.

ILSE: There's nothing wrong with my condition, but you look a bit red in the face.

KARL: It isn't how you think–

ILSE: I know.

KARL: I was showing Angie this tree.

ILSE: Grown a bit lately, has it? Last time you showed it to me it was a drooping twig.

KARL: I show Angie tree.

ANGIE: That's right, all very harmless, missus. There really is this tree. Eighteen hundred and something carved in it.

BOURKE: [*steering* ANGIE *away*] Let's get out of here before the hair and teeth start to fly.

[*They go.*]

ILSE: You think I'm stupid. When you married me, I made sure you knew what you were getting and you've hardly spoken a civil word to me since. That didn't surprise me. Nor did the nights when you would lie on me, drunk, vent your spleen inside me and roll off. Snoring. I'm carrying your child, born of a whore, you think, and fathered by a pimp. I know you. But you come laughing from the bushes with that woman wearing a shirt I washed. And you can stand there, in front of people, and tell me you were showing her a tree.

KARL: That's right.

ILSE: I'm ashamed for you.

[LEONIDS *and* RUTH *start to go.*]

KARL: Don't go. You don't have to be embarrassed for me.

LEONIDS: [*shrugging*] Lying only makes it worse.

KARL: [*angrily*] Don't you preach to me. You've worked and eaten and drunk beside a man for two years now, and all that time, right under his nose, within reach of his ears, you are rutting with his wife.

RUTH: No, Karl. Stop.

[*She cries.*]

KARL: You even helped him murder that Yank to deceive him.

LEONIDS: I never lied to his face.

KARL: No. You lie in shadows, under a tree, against a wall.

[EDVARDS *and* McQUAIDE *enter.*]

You steal from his bed in the dark while he sleeps on. Unknowing.

LEONIDS: Shut up. Shut your filthy mouth.

EDVARDS: I know. OK. I knew from the first night. I am man made. With all his imperfections. Half crazy. Half beautiful. Half ugly. And impotent. But not blind. [*To* LEONIDS] You made Ruth happy. When she left your side the warmth would steal back into my bed. From the first night you had my blessings. If you deceived yourself, you have never deceived me. If ever we killed a Yank that night in Stuttgart, we did it for Karl. For that he won't forgive his wife. He is only a small hero, our petty thief and gangster. I love him for all that. That we can stand alongside him.

[RUTH *is crying.* EDVARDS *goes to her and takes her off.* LEONIDS *goes off towards the boats.* BOURKE *enters carrying a native bark coffin.*]

BOURKE: [*excitedly*] There really is a tree. 'L eighteen hundred and–'

McQUAIDE: Yeah, I know. Otto told me.

BOURKE: What happened?

McQUAIDE: I don't know. I reckon one or two of them will be rocking a bottle tonight.

BOURKE: Say, what'd ya reckon this is?

McQUAIDE: Some old black feller's bones wrapped in bark. Let him rest in peace.

[*He tosses the bones off into the flood. They go.*]

Now we got a reason for a wake.

BOURKE: I'll drink to that.

[ILSE *and* KARL *are left alone.*]

KARL: Well? What are you waiting for?

ILSE: For you.

KARL: You're suffocating me.

ILSE: I'll go.

KARL: Not only you, the whole damn lot of you, the whole damn place. Leonids has had me by the nose for so long. If he hadn't been riding me, none of that would've come out.

ILSE: No one has to hide any more, not even you. We women don't have to pretend we don't know what happened to that G.I. in Stuttgart.

KARL: Don't you talk to me about Stuttgart.

ILSE: It's not Leonids, it's me you want to hurt. [*Crying*] And I won't cry. Not for you.

KARL: Look, I'm sorry, I'm sorry.

ILSE: That you were caught.

KARL: I didn't know you were coming up here.

ILSE: Everybody here knew what you were up to. It's only you who thinks you're the only one in the know, and you're usually the only one who isn't. It's time you grew up, I have a baby to look after.

KARL: Why don't you just throw me out?

[LEICHHARDT *enters carrying* GILBERT *on his back.*]

ILSE: That's what you'd like. To be free. No responsibilities. You think you'd be better off on your own. If you want, you'll have to stand on your own two feet and walk. I won't carry you any more.

KARL: There's nowhere to go. I'm ... I'm lost in this country. I'm afraid to go and I'm afraid to stay. My luck has deserted me. I don't know what to do.

ILSE: Stay alive like you did in Europe.

KARL: It was easy when I was by myself.

ILSE: I didn't marry you to make your life miserable or mine, and that isn't why I came to this country. I need you now, Karl.

KARL: Do you love me at all, Ilse?

ILSE: No. Not today. Maybe tomorrow I will, or in twenty years.

KARL: I never thought it would be like this. You'll drive me crazy, Ilse.

ILSE: If I came easily to you, you'd only abuse me. I'm tired now, I'm going to the camp.

KARL: Take my arm, the ground is slippery. You shouldn't be up here at all. What if you have the baby in the bush?

ILSE: The baby might feel right at home. The doctor is up here.

KARL: He's a drunk. I'll have to take you back to town.

[*They go to the camp.*]

GILBERT: Find my bones.

LEICHHARDT: You said the wild pigs took yours.

GILBERT: The pigs did take mine, but these others gave me comfort to sleep near. These intruders threw them into the flood.

LEICHHARDT: Pah! Some dried up old black woman.

GILBERT: Why have you brought me here?

LEICHHARDT: I want you to show me my tree. You are my eyes now.

GILBERT: All I see is water. Put me down. What are you up to?

LEICHHARDT: I am as innocent as when I embraced you for the last time.

GILBERT: That was just after you shot me dead. Put me down.

[GILBERT *clambers down.*]

LEICHHARDT: Your time had come. There were no blank pages left in your journal. That is past. These migrant peoples have found my marker tree. The last one. That's what I want you to show me. It is a sign of hope.

GILBERT: Of portent. They'll make no sense of it.

LEICHHARDT: Their dreams are troubled by the horrors of Europe. But they have escaped and they will forget. They are young and strong, the treasure of this country, the nucleus of a nation. And at the centre, my tree.

GILBERT: They are disaffected and wretched, not at home on this soil. Not seeing what is here, pining for what is not.

LEICHHARDT: My journey was successful.

GILBERT: The second was a failure. You died of thirst on the third. You wander still as I do. The unknown soldiers of a fruitless battle, inevitably lost.

LEICHHARDT: What could you be but a pessimist, forever gazing into the gutses of dead things? Show me my tree. There is life, and then I will find your bones.

GILBERT: I will find them myself.

LEICHHARDT: I will carry you through the water.

GILBERT: I don't trust you.

[GILBERT *walks into the flood.*]

LEICHHARDT: Wait, wait.

GILBERT: Don't worry. Your position is firmly mapped in my mind.

[*And he's gone.*]

LEICHHARDT: You can't desert me now. Come back.

[RUTH *enters. She is drawn to the boats.*]

RUTH: [*calling softly*] Leonids.

EDVARDS: Ruthie.

[RUTH *goes to him.*]

I am so tired.

RUTH: You work too hard. Lie down. Put your head in my lap.

[*He does.*]

EDVARDS: Leonids is not a bad man.

RUTH: Hush!

EDVARDS: You won't ever leave me?

RUTH: Go to sleep.

EDVARDS: We all work hard. We are all good men, in our own way.

[LEONIDS *enters.*]

RUTH: He's asleep.

LEONIDS: It won't be the same now. I can't stay.

[RUTH *nods.*]

Come with me.

RUTH: Back to town? That's nowhere. They'd follow.

LEONIDS: We'll take one of the boats. Go down river. I have everything we need. I've saved a lot of money. We can start afresh together.

[RUTH *gently lowers* EDVARDS *head. She goes with* LEONIDS. EDVARDS *stirs.*]

EDVARDS: [*as though in a dream*] Can't touch her. Can't stop her. I could scream. I can only watch her go.

[*He wakes as the boat's motor starts and sits up.*]

Ruth! Leonids! Wait! Wait! Take me with you. You can't desert me now. Come back. Come back!

[ILSE *and* KARL *come running.* KARL *drags him back.*]

KARL: Edvards, what the hell ...

EDVARDS: She's gone. Let me go.

[*The others come.*]

McQUAIDE: Is he all right?

KARL: Yes. The boat. Leonids and Ruth.

McQUAIDE: My boat's gone. They took my boat. [*To* BOURKE] Go after them.

EDVARDS: [*taking* BOURKE *towards his boat*] Ruth. Take me. Find Ruth. Take me.

BOURKE: Stop him. There's only enough petrol to get back to town.

KARL: No petrol, Edvards.

EDVARDS: I work contract. Work hard. No pay. You find Ruth.

[EDVARDS *charges off.*]

BOURKE: Where's he goin' now? We'll all have to go back to town. They'll send out a search party.

ILSE: Ruthie.

KARL: Leonids. Don't be stupid.

[*The sound of chopping starts, off. Full-blooded swings with an axe.*]

BOURKE: What is he doing?

OTTO: Edvards working.

KARL: He's cutting down that old tree.

BOURKE: Bloody hell. We gotta stop that.

LEICHHARDT: [*off*] Stop! Stop! Are you mad! Crazy swine!

[*All go except* ILSE.]

ILSE: Ruth!

[*The chopping continues.*]

SCENE FIVE

North Queensland, 1949. Night.

ILSE *is in labour.* RUTH *enters. By this light she looks much as she did in the last scene. Her hair is a little wilder.*

ILSE: Ruth! You've come again tonight.

RUTH: I said last night I would.

ILSE: Where have you been?

RUTH: I walked until it grew too windy. It's still flooding. Does it hurt, Ilse?

ILSE: Yes. Horribly. Sometimes. [*Talking through a contraction*] I have hurt worse before and I know that this will pass. At times I think the pain will never end and I will die. How cold your hand is.

[RUTH *draws her hand away.*]

RUTH: My hands used to be soft and supple. Now they are stiff and puffy and white. I use a cream, but I've run out. Lend me yours.

ILSE: You know my hands. Like slabs of meat. I don't use a cream. And it shows.

[*An owl calls.* RUTH *starts.*]

RUTH: Look what's happened. My hair is a mess. Lend me your brush.

ILSE: I can't.

RUTH: I'm going away, Ilse, with Leonids. I have nothing to wear. The moths have eaten my clothes. What isn't eaten, green mould grows on, like moss. Give me your shawl.

ILSE: No.

RUTH: You'll never wear it again. You'll have more children, settle here and never go back home. You don't need the shawl. Give it to me.

ILSE: No. Please go.

RUTH: Can't you see how unhappy I am? I have a pain in my heart, Ilse.

ILSE: [*crying*] And do you think I don't?

RUTH: I'm not asking for much. A tiny silver spoon will do.

ILSE: It's for the christening.

RUTH: There will be others. A keepsake, Ilse.

ILSE: I'll always remember you. I love you.

RUTH: Help me! Ilse, I can't catch my breath. Help me!

ILSE: No, too late. Far too late. I can give you nothing. To give you something, however paltry, is to take from the life of my child. [*Moaning*] He is kicking and butting to get out. I love you, Ruthie, I love you.

[KARL *enters.*]

KARL: The doctor is coming. You're crying. I'll make him hurry.

ILSE: No! Stay with me.

[KARL *sits on the bed. A brief pause.*]

KARL: [*to* ILSE] They found the boat. Washed up. Miles away. That's all. They must have drowned.

[*He puts his head on the bed and cries.*]

RUTH: Goodbye, Ilse.

[*She goes.*]

ILSE: Ruth was here.

KARL: [*lifting his head*] Another dream. You're a real peasant, you are.

ILSE: [*taking his hand and putting it on her stomach*] Feel! Don't look so afraid. He's just anxious to see this country of his.

KARL: Or hers. Could be a daughter. I'll try to do the right thing. For once.

SCENE SIX

North Queensland, 1950. Day.

LEICHHARDT: It is believed in Sydney that I have been murdered long ago, or that I have starved to death. I am curious what people will say when I appear suddenly, resurrected from the grave, with a heap of mountain ranges and rivers in my pockets.

GILBERT: People will be astonished at my beautiful collection. Never before will they have seen skins got up in such style.

LEICHHARDT: I fear I will be so affected in finding myself again in civilised society, that I will scarcely be able to speak. In my throat the words will grow big with tears and emotion.

[LYDIA *and* ILSE *enter, separate from* KARL *and* OTTO. LYDIA *holds the child wrapped in the shawl.*]

ILSE: Hurry now. You don't want to miss your train.

LYDIA: Come with us. Come to Sydney. Life will be better. I don't know how you can stay ...

[*She trails off.*]

ILSE: In the city I'd think of Ruth and Leonids more. I'd see them in the streets, believing they got away safely.

[KARL *and* OTTO *join* EDVARDS. RUTH *stands with* LEONIDS.]

KARL: We're brothers. We ate together, got drunk together, slept with women–

EDVARDS: And we killed men together. Joined by blood.

OTTO: Ssh! You'll get me into trouble. If ever you come to Sydney–

KARL: I'd like to be going now.

OTTO: What will you do?

KARL: Become a peasant. Scratch a living from the ground. I'll always wonder if I made a mistake. I was making a nice living in Germany and maybe I should have gone to America.

EDVARDS: Poor Karl is still in shock about not going to Hollywood. OK. He has Australian nightmares instead of American dreams.

LYDIA: There's nobody left for you to talk to, except Karl and Edvards.

ILSE: I'll talk to the people who live here.

LYDIA: An outsider can't hope to understand this society. It's different if you're born here. You'll only be welcome at the bottom.

ILSE: [*not unkindly*] And you will go to Sydney and collect in pockets with other Latvians. You'll be a crutch to each other and dream for ever of returning home.

KARL: I still do. Don't you?

ILSE: I dream. But this place is so unlike home, I can make a new life.

[*She takes the child.*]

See, I've started–

LEONIDS: The train is coming.

RUTH: At last we are going.

LEONIDS: In those last few days before we left Stuttgart, I imagined that at any moment an American provo would take me away and you would all leave without me.

ILSE: I won't go to the train. It'll disturb the baby. Goodbye, Lydia.

[*They embrace lightly.*]

LYDIA: I'll write. You must come and see us. Goodbye.

OTTO: [*giving a handshake and a kiss*] Goodbye, Ilse.

KARL: I'll come over with you.

[*The train comes to a halt. Doors open and close. The guard's whistle blows. The train pulls away.*]

RUTH: Oh Leonids. We're truly lost then.

LEONIDS: I'd just hoped we'd catch the train and get off somewhere, just as we'd planned.

RUTH: We'll never get away now or find any peace.

LEONIDS: I'm sorry Ruthie.

[ILSE *softly sings 'Blow Breeze' to the baby.* KARL *walks back from the train.*]

LEICHHARDT: All has passed before me now like a vivid dream. The remnants are only a few impressions, satisfied vanity, and the memory of some graceful girl.

KARL: I won't be able to call this place home. Not for a long time.

ILSE: Don't drink too much and save your money. You have a daughter to take care of. I will work too.

THE END